MILITANT NICE GUY

MILITANT
NICE
GUY

Using Your Nice Guy Tendencies To Your Advantage

Terrance Terry

Terrance Terry   *Militant Nice Guy: Using Your Nice Guy Tendencies to Your Advantage*

Author's note: Events described in this book happened as remembered. Names have been changed to respect privacy and anonymity.

Library of Congress Cataloging-in-publication Data

Terry, Terrance

p.   cm.

I. Interpersonal Relationships II. Communication III. Self Development
HF 5387 L66 2015   646.78 TE

ISBN: 978-0-9906120-3-2

Printed in the United States of America

CONTENTS

Why You Fear Your Negative Emotions
How Your Negative Emotions Give You Your Integrity
Jerks and Their Negative Emotions
How Negative Emotions Keep You From Deluding Yourself
How Listening To Your Negative Emotions Can Help You
Implementing/Using Your Negative Emotions
Another Example of Implementation of Negative Emotions

INTRODUCTION

I bet I know something about you. I bet that you do not like it when a woman calls you a "nice guy." That is because you think being a Nice Guy is a bad thing, and if you do, then you are entirely justified in thinking so.

Let's take a look at some of what it means to be a Nice Guy for so many people:

Jerks stealing your women

Constantly being put in the "friend zone"

Being ineffective with women

Being unable to generate sexual interest from women

Having a lack of confidence

Feeling misunderstood

☢

These are among the many reasons why so many people think it is a bad thing for you to be a nice guy. What if I told you that it doesn't have to be this way for you anymore? What if I told you that being a nice guy no longer has to be a burden, and that it can actually be a good thing to be nice? The reason I can say this is because I now believe I know what is working against you and nice guys like you, I know what keeps you from being an effective and efficient nice guy. There is a reason why you are not proud to be a nice guy. It is because we live in a society that encourages you to repress your nice guy tendencies, and makes you ashamed to be a nice guy. You may have heard expressions such as:

Don't be so nice

Nice Guys finish last

Nice Guys do not stand up for themselves

Women don't want a Nice Guy

Being nice only gets you stuck in the friend zone

Nice Guys are not strong

Nice Guys are weak

Nice Guys are not sexy

Many nice guys not only accept these expressions as true, but many have also taken part in endorsing, and spreading these beliefs about nice guys to others. Now, if you call yourself a nice guy and you share these beliefs, then what does this say about how you see yourself? Another important question for you is: Why would a woman ever want a nice guy if she is constantly reminded by you, and others, that you are the romantically inferior option? What you are doing is working against yourself, and destroying your self-esteem. It is extremely difficult for you to be proud of who you are if you feel this way about yourself as a nice guy.

If you are a nice guy, then you are the reason I decided to call this book Militant Nice Guy. The word "militant" is usually used to mean vigorously active and aggressive, especially in support of a cause. The cause that I vigorously, actively, and aggressively support, is you being a better nice guy. I wrote this book to give you a new way to look at yourself, where being a Nice Guy is something to be proud of.

Militant Nice Guy has four major goals:
1. To show you what is working against you; what is keeping you from using your Nice Guy tendencies to your advantage.
2. To help you to use your Nice Guy tendencies to make you a more efficient and effective communicator.
3. To help arm you with more efficient methods for dealing with the "Jerk."
4. To examine, challenge, and test your perception of what it means to be a Nice Guy

When I first started writing this book, I was concerned with how I could make sure the information herein is used responsibly. The last thing I want is for someone to take the information in this book and misuse it.

This is how I overcame my fear:

I was watching a television interview of a martial arts instructor who was teaching children how to defend themselves from being picked on by bullies. The instructor was asked, "How do you keep the children from using their new-found martial-arts skills to bully other kids? How do you keep the kids from turning into bullies themselves?" He explained that he not only gives them the skills to fight, but he gives them the rules, conditions, and parameters for using their skills. Because of this, he believes that anything they do with their skills after he gives them the knowledge then becomes the students' responsibility.

So in that spirit, let's start by looking at what this book is not:

This book is not about turning you in to a Jerk, which would defeat its purpose. A Nice Guy has an inherent number of excellent traits and characteristics of his own, which makes him very attractive. The issue is that the average Nice Guy does not know what these traits are, or how to use them effectively.

This book is not necessarily focused on teaching you how to understand or "get" women.

The reason why women are discussed so extensively in this book is because Nice Guys often see themselves through the eyes of women. They judge themselves based on what they think her standards and beliefs are, and not through their own personal Nice Guy standards and beliefs. Besides, what is the point of understanding women if you do not understand yourself?

☢

This information is not about stealing another man's woman.

Once she is committed to another man, then all bets are off. Even if she is committed to some Jerk who is treating her horribly, as far as *Militant Nice Guy* is concerned, she is off limits to you.

This book is not a quick fix or a magic bullet.

This book is primarily focused on examining the Nice Guy mindset, why he thinks the way he thinks and what causes him to think this way, and that is an extensive process that is far from being a quick fix.

This book is not intended to be the only way to be a better Nice Guy.

There are many ways to be a better Nice Guy, this book is one of many. The topics, concepts, and information in *Militant Nice Guy* are not to be set in stone; it is not meant to be the last word on the subject.

It is only meant to be a starting point so that we are all on the same page when it comes to examining the issues that concerns Nice Guys.

Militant Nice Guy offers a perspective to help Nice Guys use their Nice Guy tendencies to their advantage; it does not necessarily claim to offer standard "one size fits all" answers or solutions to specific situations. This is because the problem with one size fits all solutions is that for every situation where the standard answer or solution works, there are at least a dozen where it does not work. *Militant Nice Guy* was written to examine some of the major issues that concern the Nice Guy. This examination is so that you can understand the problems concerning Nice Guys and the principles behind how those problems work.

When you understand the principles behind the problems, then it will be much easier to come up with your own solutions and answers for yourself, which fit your particular situation. This is an important part of you becoming a more effective Nice Guy. The information in this book is only a tool for you to use and adapt to your own particular set of circumstances.

☢

Militant Nice Guy is divided into three main sections:

In the **first** section, *Militant Nice Guy* will examine the outside factors at work against the Nice Guy. And will show you how this has made the Nice Guy ineffective.

In the **second** section, we will examine who the Nice Guy is, and how these outside factors have distorted how the Nice Guy sees himself.

In the **third** section, we will examine how the Nice Guy interacts with others as a result of his lack of belief in himself.

CHAPTER ONE

THE CONSPIRACY AGAINST THE NICE GUY

What is Working Against You

Think about how many times you have lost a woman you either wanted or were seeing to some Jerk because you believed you were "too nice." When this happened, I know you stayed awake many nights wondering many things, such as:

> How could she have chosen that Jerk over you?
> What the hell is going on?
> Why can't she see how good you are for her?
> What is wrong with you?
> What is wrong with her?
> Why does she keep leaving you for the Jerk?
> What does the Jerk know that you don't?

How many female friends do you have or women do you know who seem to keep falling for Jerk after Jerk, over and over again. This confuses and frustrates many Nice Guys, because women say they want a Nice Guy, and seem to intellectually understand Jerks are bad for them. But if that is true, then why do they keep going back to the Jerk so predictably? What is it about these Jerks that women find so irresistible?

I believe a strong argument can be made that the number one question most Nice Guys have for women is: Why do women all over the world constantly reject someone so obviously good for them for someone so obviously bad for them? If these women could just tell us why, maybe we as Nice Guys could have some peace. I know I am not the first Nice Guy to ask these questions. Many people before me have asked this question. As a matter of fact, there are already many answers to this question.

Common Theories as to Why Women Reject Nice Guys for Jerks
Women are:

Crazy	Stupid
Into being dominated	Don't know any better
Easy prey	Unintelligent
Liars	Whores
Confused	Sluts
Followers	Really into Jerks
Naturally attracted to Jerks	Excited by the challenge

While these answers may be valid and important, they somehow seem unsatisfying and incomplete, especially for the Nice Guy. Doesn't it feel like there is something more going on? Doesn't it almost seems as if there is a mysterious force working against you and Nice Guys like you that is keeping you from getting and/or keeping the women you want, (especially when there is a Jerk involved in the picture)? It's almost as if she can't help herself, it seems like the worse the guy, the stronger her attraction is to him? Why is that? Doesn't if feel like those Jerks out there know some secret you do not? Don't you feel like something suspicious is going on?

Let me ask you this: how many times have you wondered why being a Nice Guy automatically puts you at a disadvantage with women when you are competing with the Jerk? Why does it seem as if women are only attracted to a certain type of guy; and that guy is not you? Doesn't it almost feel as if the game is rigged against you? I no longer think that this is by chance; I believe this is happening on purpose. I believe you have been manipulated to accept and believe in the "so-called" inferior position of the Nice Guy.

☢

The Conspiracy and You

I believe there is a "Conspiracy" working against you to keep you from being proud of who you are as a Nice Guy. I believe this is an extensive and far reaching Conspiracy. What the Conspiracy wants is to control you by making you doubt yourself. The Conspiracy does this by stealing your confidence and by destroying your belief in yourself. The

Conspiracy is all around you, from the books you read, to the music you listen to, to the movies and programs on you watch television. It even extends to the very people you chose to associate with every day. You may even be a part of spreading the Conspiracy and do not even know it. Those behind the Conspiracy do this by doing their best to convince you, and others that being a Nice Guy is a bad thing, especially when it comes to interacting efficiently and effectively with women.

Now you may be asking: Why would someone go through all this trouble to damage you as a Nice Guy? What is the point of the Conspiracy? What is the end goal? The goal of the Conspiracy is to make you irrelevant when it comes to dating and women, so that the Jerks can have all of the women for themselves.

The Conspiracy does this by portraying the Nice Guy as the "inferior option" when it comes to dating and women. They want people, especially women, to see the Nice Guy as a good friend, companion, brotherly, anything else other than a viable romantic/sexual option when compared to the Jerk. Has the Conspiracy has infected you?

Some signs you may be infected by the Conspiracy
You do not feel worthy of a woman's attention
You feel constant anxiety around women
You are jealous of Jerks
You believe women prefer Jerks
You hesitate to approach women you are interested in
You believe Jerks are naturally more desirable than Nice Guys

It is not that Jerks are naturally superior to you or deserve these women any more than you do; it is just that they have a whole system in place dedicated to stopping you, which gives the advantage to the Jerk. That system is the Conspiracy.

I want to expose the Conspiracy to you for two reasons:
One: Because I am one of you, a Nice Guy, I know the pain of constantly losing women to Jerks over and over again. I know all about the

danger taking of all those rejections personally. We all know what it is like to be called "nice" by a woman and then experience that sinking feeling because you think you know exactly what that means. If being called a Nice Guy is suppose to be so great, then why does it feel so bad to be called that? I truly believe I now have an answer to that question. I also believe I can offer you a unique insight and perspective to your situation.

Two: If there is any group of people who need to have a better understanding of who they are and a sense of pride in themselves, then it is Nice Guys. I sympathize with Nice Guys because all they want is to do right by themselves and by the women in their lives. It angers me to see them targeted for manipulation for no reason other than they are in the way of Jerks who want these women for themselves. I believe if I can help Nice Guys feel better about themselves, then it will help save them from some unnecessary pain and suffering.

Now I understand that there are some people reading this book who will not accept the theory of the Conspiracy. That is understandable. It took me a very long time before I was fully able to understand and accept the idea of the Conspiracy, so for all those skeptics I know how you feel. Fortunately, for all involved, the information in this book will help to make you a more effective Nice Guy whether you believe in the Conspiracy or not.

How I Discovered the Conspiracy

I actually discovered the Conspiracy by accident. I started on my path to discovery when I met James. James was confusing to me, by confusing I mean he treated women horribly. It appeared that the worse he treated them, the more women loved him for it. I have always hated James; he was the stereotypical lazy bum who never had a job and was generally unpleasant to be around. He thought he was better than everyone else because he could get women to do whatever he wanted them to do. This was bothersome to me because women loved him and all he did was treat them poorly. It was both disgusting and fascinating at the same time to watch woman after woman just give themselves, their time, affection, and their money to this creep. These were very desirable women; most were good looking, professional, smart and had a lot going for themselves.

So one day. out of sheer frustration and burning curiosity, I decided to ask James what his secret was to getting these women to do whatever he wanted. I was shocked by what he told me. He bragged to me that his secret was where he met the women. He told me he would meet these women at science and business expos, medical and engineering conventions, anywhere where high-level professional people congregate. I said, "But you don't have a job and barely finished high school, how can you compete with all of the other professional men there?" What he told next simply blew my mind:

He said, "I don't have to worry about those professional guys. See, it is very likely the men who are in highly professional jobs like doctors, scientists, businessmen, and especially engineers, were the "smart" Nice Guys in school." He went on to say, "It does not matter to me that these guys are now grown, professional, and are well-paid. It's like some mysterious force out there has done all of the work for me before I even showed up to talk to these women. These intelligent Nice Guys have known since high school that they were no good with women and they have spent their entire adult lives thinking that. That won't change just because they now have some money. All I have to do is walk in the room, venue, or convention, and once I see all of those smart Nice Guys with all their money and resources, I know that they have lost the game before they have even started playing. All I have to do is just walk in and take the women I want because I know these Nice Guys won't even walk up and talk to them. Even if they do, they will be so awkward and painful, that it makes me look like an even better option to the woman."

I told him that I could not believe that he just walks into these professional environments with no job, education, or resources, and gets these women.

"Why not?" He told me, "I have been stealing hot chicks from Nice Guys since the ninth grade. I don't see any difference with these guys just because they are now adults. I don't see doctors, scientist, or engineers, I just see Nice Guys with resources. A rich Nice Guy is still just a Nice Guy to me. I am not worried about not having a job, or being on their level financially because it does not matter. When it comes to how I get women, I don't have to be the best guy there, I just have to be the best out of all the guys talking to the women, and no one is talking to them but me. It's just like in high school. People don't just change who they are because they now have money. Money doesn't make you who you are; it is a reflection of who you are, and these guys are weak."

My first thought was, *Oh my goodness; what a horrible person*. However, if I were honest with myself, I would also have to admit there was some truth in what he was saying.

When he said: "It seems as if some mysterious force is out there helping me," I did not realize it at the time, but those words he spoke, helped set me on the path to expose the Conspiracy towards Nice Guys. At the time I did not fully understand it, but I started to look around and examine things from that perspective, and was amazed at what I found.

Going Deeper into the Conspiracy

I wanted to see if this revelation I discovered with James was an isolated incident or if I had accidentally stumbled on to some hidden truth about Nice Guys by talking to him. I wanted to see if other Jerks thought like him and had the same experiences that he did. So what I decided to do was to informally interview other Jerks to see what I would find. The reason I decided to talk to Jerks was because I believed understanding the point of view of the Jerk was crucial to me understanding exactly what the Nice Guy is up against.

When it comes to understanding Jerks, you can only gain so much information from looking at the aftermath of how the Jerk mistreats women, or by talking to the Nice Guy who lost his woman to the Jerk. If you only look at things from the Nice Guy's perspective, and/or the female perspective, then you would never fully understand what the Jerk was thinking, or his motivations. I decided I needed to talk to as many Jerks as I could find to understand their perspectives, motivations, and what was going on in their heads. I did not know at the time how significant this little project would be to my life and for Nice Guys in general.

It would make sense to ask: "Why would Jerks want to talk to you about how bad they treat women?" I wondered this myself in the beginning. One of the main things I had going for me with this project was the fact that they had no idea they were being interviewed. I would often come to them as a kindred spirit, as if I was someone who believed in and supported their actions. More often than not, that was normally all it took to get them to open up.

There are other major reasons why I think the Jerks themselves wanted to talk with me about their interactions. Many did not see themselves as doing anything wrong; so why not to talk about their interactions? Some wanted to get their side of the story out. This was true especially if they were accused of doing something especially bad. Some wanted to share what they did because they were proud of their actions.

I wanted whatever information the Jerks had to tell me, but I was primarily looking for answers to four basic questions: Why did you pick the woman you picked? What did you do to get her? What did you think about her as a woman? What do you think of the Nice Guy she is seeing, and do you think you are in competition with him?

After I conducted only ten of these informal interviews, I knew I was on to something. For the first time in my life I was able to correlate what was going on in the Jerks' heads with what influences they had on women. The more interviews I did, the more confident I began to feel there was something working against the Nice Guy. While the interviews with these Jerks were eye-opening in and of themselves, I was also able to compare notes on the various Jerks, and I noticed certain trends and reoccurring themes.

The Jerk had no idea that I was taking his answers and comparing them to what other Jerks said. I could compare what he said to what he actually did. I could hear what he thought about the woman and the Nice Guy she was involved with when it was relevant. These interviews were crucial to me understanding how a Jerk thinks and how he uses his power to defeat you as a Nice Guy. This is what set me on the path to uncover and expose what the Conspiracy has done to you.

☢

Who is Behind the Conspiracy

As for the identity of those who are behind the Conspiracy, this book is not the format for this topic. The identity of those behind the Conspiracy could easily take up two other books. This book is about what the Conspiracy has done to the Nice Guy, and this book is about using your Nice Guy tendencies to your advantage.

If you are laying in the emergency room shot, the doctor treating you does not ask you to describe the person who shot you. This is because it does not matter who shot you when it comes to treatment. The treatment is the same regardless of who has shot you, and weather you were shot by accident or on purpose. It is the same with the Conspiracy against the Nice Guy, identification of who is behind the Conspiracy is not the primary concern of Militant Nice Guy; the treatment is what matters.

The Two Levels of the Conspiracy

The Conspiracy is actively working against the Nice Guy on two different levels.

The first level we will examine has to do with how the Conspiracy controls how the Nice Guy thinks. The Conspiracy has succeeded in filling the Nice Guy with doubt and shame when it comes to him going after what he wants, and how he sees himself as a Nice Guy. What the Conspiracy has done is taken the Nice Guy's thoughts, perceptions, and natural Nice Guy tendencies and turned them against him, especially when he interacts with women. This is a major reason why many Nice Guys are often satisfied with other areas of their life, except for when it come to interacting with women, because he does not believe in and trust his Nice Guy tendencies romantically and sexually.

The second level we will examine is how the Conspiracy has created a culture of misinformation against the Nice Guy. This is where we will look at how the Conspiracy has force-fed the Nice Guy propaganda, which in addition to convincing him not to like himself, it also makes him inefficient at expressing himself. This culture of misinformation not only controls how the Nice Guy sees himself, but also how others see the Nice Guy. This culture of misinformation is a big reason why most of the advice available to Nice Guys does not work for them. This is because the advice usually comes from someone who either does not know what it means to be a Nice Guy, does not like Nice Guys, or does not understands Nice Guys. But before we get too deep into how the Conspiracy has corrupted Nice Guys like you, let's look at what the Conspiracy has done to damage Nice Guys' self-esteem.

What the Conspiracy Has Done to Your Self-esteem

The thing that makes conspiracies so effective is that they do not need your approval or even your knowledge of the conspiracy for you to be manipulated by it. As stated earlier, the Conspiracy wants to take out their competition, which is you, and Nice Guys like you. They have done a pretty good job of it so far. The way the Conspiracy takes you out is through neutralization. You are neutralized in two different ways: doubt and shame. These are two very important reasons why you do not trust yourself and/or have a poor self-image of yourself as a Nice Guy.

The Conspiracy has systematically put propaganda out there about you and Nice Guys like you with the express purpose of filling you with doubt and shame. When you experience doubt and/or shame, it causes your interactions to be less effective. If you believe you are not worthy to talk to her, do not have the skill, or that some Jerk will show up and take the woman you want, then you will be much less likely to take action; or the action you do take will be half-hearted and timid. This will make it even less likely that you will take action in the future. It is a vicious cycle, and this is the major way you are neutralized. With you out of the way, the woman will have no choice but to deal with the Jerk.

☢

Why You Doubt Yourself

Doubt is the opposite of confidence. You experience self-doubt when you do not have faith in your abilities to succeed in what you are doing, or about to do. The Conspiracy has trained the Nice Guy not only to doubt himself excessively, it also makes the Nice Guy believe that something is wrong with him for having this doubt.

Let's first start with how the Conspiracy turns your doubt against you. Think back to all the times you saw a beautiful woman you wanted to talk to, but you were afraid to approach her. You know the women I am talking about, the ones who look so good they make your knees buckle. It is even hard to look them in the face because they are so beautiful.

Now pick one of these women from your past and ask yourself, why did you not talk to her? Maybe you felt, like she was just a little bit out of your league, or maybe you believed that you didn't deserve her. Were you filled with doubt because you did not know what to do around her? Perhaps you had issues with coming up with something to say to her, or maybe you were trying to think of a way to get her to like you? Whatever the reason, you wanted to say something to her but you did not because you experienced doubt.

You experienced doubt because when you saw her, you thought back to all the other times you were nervous around women you were considering approaching. You thought back to all of the other times you wanted to say something to a woman but could not come up with anything good enough to say. You remember how badly things went for you when you did decide to talk to women like her, and you do not want to go through that again. This is understandable. If you normally have a history of little or no success with situations like this, then it is no wonder this is the conclusion you would draw when presented with another.

Your doubt is a major reason why you do nothing. You hesitate because you doubt your ability to consistently engage in successful interactions with women. Well your doubt is well earned my friend. Your doubt is based on something; your doubt is based on reason; your doubt comes from somewhere familiar. Where does yours come from? For most Nice Guys, their doubt comes in large part from constant rejection, and what really magnifies' the Nice Guy's doubt is: "Jerk rejection."

What is "Jerk rejection"? It is when a woman not only rejects you outright, but rejects you for an inferior product, that inferior product being the Jerk. To be honest, most Nice Guys can deal with a woman rejecting them outright. That rejection, while disappointing, is understandable. Actually, most Nice Guys can even deal with a woman he wants picking another worthy guy over him. It doesn't feel good, but he can usually get over it because he can at least understand what happened: he simply lost her to someone else who was a worthy contender.

What really breaks a Nice Guy's heart and keeps him up at nights with both fist raised toward the sky screaming, "Why!!??" (like a scene from a movie), is when a woman chooses a major Jerk over him. Often, it goes well beyond her making a simple mistake of choosing the wrong guy. The guy she usually picks over the Nice Guy leaves him wanting to look her deep in her eyes asking: "How in the hell can you not see that choosing that Jerk will turn out very badly for you". When she rejects the Nice Guy for the Jerk, it is like injecting steroids into the Nice Guy's doubt.

The following example perfectly illustrates this point: My friend Alan and I were going to an exclusive party where I had a pair of all-access passes. I told him he was in luck because the party we were going to was a cowboy party where all the women there love cowboys. Alan is a real deal cowboy who lives on a ranch with cows, horses and pigs, an actual cowboy. I told him all he had to do was let the women at the party know that he was a real cowboy, and he was in. He was really excited because he knew it was going to be a good night. He wore his cowboy hat, his favorite cowboy boots, and jeans.

At the party, he approached some women and told him about being a cowboy. Then boom, he gets rejected. *No big deal,* he thinks, *I am a cowboy, this is a cowboy party, and women here love cowboys. There must be something wrong with her, no big deal.* So he strolled up to another woman and got rejected again. I saw what was happening. He came over to me to ask for some advice, but I was clueless. I had absolutely nothing for him, so I gave him the same advice most people give when they have nothing of any practical value. I told him there was nothing to fear but fear itself, be positive, and go up to the women. "Be confident and say hello," I reiterated. So he walked confidently up to another group of women, and boom, he gets blown out again.

Alan started to look around the party and saw that some rappers were getting all the attention. He was confused, and thought, *I thought this was a cowboy party. The women say they are here for cowboys, and I am a cowboy, so what gives? And what the hell are rappers doing at a cowboy party anyway?*

He tried talking to more and more women, and one by one he sees their attention going to the rappers.

Now Alan has very little choice but to come to one of two conclusions:

1. He can take all of these rejections personally:

He could conclude: *The women say they want a cowboy, and I am a cowboy, but I keep getting rejected. It is logical for me to conclude that they do not like me personally because there must be something wrong with me.*

2. Assume they do not want a cowboy and want the rappers:

He could conclude: *The women do not like the cowboys, they like the rappers. Since I am a cowboy, I will never get a woman at this party.*

With either choice or both, Alan concludes that the women at that party do not want him. Alan now has doubt. He doubts that the rest of the night will go well. He doubts there are any women at the party who want him. He doubts he will have any success with the women at the party. He doubts that rappers are having as much of a problem as he is with these women. He doubts being a cowboy will ever work out for him as long as he is at that party. He has doubts because he does not know what to do and/or how to proceed with these women. His doubts about his success about that night have been earned from his previous experience with the women at that party, and no amount of positive thinking can change that.

Fortunately for Alan, his feeling of doubt will start to go away as soon he leaves that party because he knows that party was an isolated incident. But unfortunately for most Nice Guys who feel the same way Alan felt at that party, those feeling of doubt never go away. Nice Guys doubt themselves because they are reminded of their past failures and they see their past failure as justification for their doubt. Their past failures magnify their perfectly natural fear of rejection. Often, because of this, he may start to think of himself as flawed or start to develop an inferiority complex, especially relative to the Jerk.

☢

Why You Feel Shame

Whether you take your rejections personally or not, there is one thing that you will have a hard time denying: It's really hard to keep these constant rejections from instilling doubt in you. You doubt your ability to initiate and/or have a successful romantic and/or sexual relationship with women. How can you think anything else, especially when you believe your own personal history has shown you otherwise? When we experience constant doubt it can often lead to shame.

Shame, as far as *Militant Nice Guy* is concerned, is how you feel about yourself because of your doubt and your perceived inefficiencies. You feel shame because of constantly being rejected by women. That shame is greatly magnified when she constantly rejects you for a Jerk who you think is much worse for her than you. It is easy to see why you would think something is wrong with you. As a result, you could start to blame your lack of success with women on the fact that you are a Nice Guy.

You are embarrassed because you do not know how to be effective with women, you feel as if you should be able to handle this part of your life better. This constant rejection has frustrated many Nice Guys for many different reasons, but the main one *Militant Nice Guy* will focus on is a lack of control.

This is where shame comes in. You think something is wrong with you, and you don't know why. You don't know how to fix it, and it frustrates you, because you do not know how to keep it from happening to you again. You feel shame because you seem to have no control over this part of your life. You just want the rejections to stop, or at least gain an understanding as to why you are constantly being rejected.

One of the most common solutions for Nice Guys is to avoid situations where they might have a chance of being hurt like that again. This often means not talking to women who look like they may hurt you the way you were hurt before. This is a big reason why you hesitate when you see a woman you are interested in across the room. You hesitate because you feel fear. You feel fear because you think the interaction will go badly. You think it will go badly because you feel as if you have either very little or no control or influence in making your interaction a success. This is in large part because this is how it has been for you in the past, and/or how you have seen it go for other Nice Guys. That is why you do nothing. And that is how you are neutralized.

The following is a perfect example of how neutralization of the Nice Guy works. My friend grew up with a neighbor who was a dog lover and he would show up every six months or so with a new stray dog that he would get from the dog pound or shelter. Now he didn't like dogs. Why? Because when he was a little kid, he heard those fateful last words: "Go ahead and pet him, he won't bite." I think we all know how that worked out for him.

Whenever my neighbor would get another dog from the pound, my friend could always tell which dogs were abused and beaten. Because whenever someone would try to get too close to him, all he would have to do is pretend as if he was reaching down to the ground to pick up something to throw at the dog, and it would run away, even though he had nothing in his hand. Most of the dogs ran away with their heads down and tails between their legs. This happened with dog after dog; it was a very accurate indicator for me of which dogs had been abused.

Now the question is, why would the dogs just run away like that? It is because they could not tell that he wouldn't do anything to hurt them. They ran because as far as the dogs were concerned, they were in a situation similar to ones where they have been hurt many times before. If they see any situation that remotely looks like it may hurt them as they have been hurt before, then they very smartly won't take any chances; they just get out of there as fast as they can.

Most Nice Guys are like that abused dog. The difference is Nice Guys have been abused with rejection, misinformation, and self-doubt. As a result, most Nice Guys don't like themselves, because they feel as if they have no control over their situation, and they feel helpless.

In order to keep the same disappointing rejection from happening to him again and again, many Nice Guys will try to look for other ways to interact with women to avoid rejection.

Some common ways Nice Guys try to avoid/deal with rejection:
 Trying to be someone/something he is not

 Trying to control/dominate her

 Overcompensating

 Trying to pretend he does not like her to get her

 Supplicating/doing whatever she wants

 Trying to get a friend to act on his behalf

 Acting as if he wants something else from her in order to hide his interest in her

Most Nice Guys have tried these methods (and many others), and they are often proven to be ineffective. The reason why is because none of these methods take into account what the Conspiracy has done to the

Nice Guy. The Conspiracy loves it when a Nice Guy experiences constant rejection, especially when a woman chooses a Jerk over him. This is because it knows constant rejection makes the Nice Guy confused, and vulnerable, to the next part of the Conspiracy's plan.

CHAPTER TWO

THE CULTURE OF MISINFORMATION

To Be a Nice Guy or Not to Be a Nice Guy

Confusion is a wonderful tool to use when you want to manipulate someone, and the Conspiracy has succeeded magnificently in causing great confusion in Nice Guys. They want to confuse us, because when we are confused about who we are, and what we want, then we will be very hesitant to take action.

Misinformation is a major part of the Conspiracy's plan to neutralize the Nice Guy. The Conspiracy has created a culture of misinformation to control not only how you see yourself, but it also controls how the world see you. A major part of the Conspiracy's plan to confuse you is by distorting yourself image of what it means to be a Nice Guy.

Nice Guys receive conflicting information on not only what it means to be a Nice Guy, but also on how the Nice Guy is supposed to behave. What is especially sinister is the Conspiracy often gives Nice Guys conflicting and confusing information on weather not or it is even beneficial at all to be a Nice Guy. This propaganda is everywhere. It is a safe bet that even you, at times, might have (unknowingly) taken part in the Conspiracy's plan to neutralize you by having you send your own mixed messages about Nice Guys.

We live in a culture that says one thing about being a Nice Guy, and then it turns around and says the exact opposite.

We live in a culture that says:	*Then says:*
Treat women with respect	Nice Guys finish last
Women want to marry the Nice Guy	You have to be a Jerk get ahead
Be positive	Women want bad boys
Be considerate	Women want a guy with an edge
Women like the Nice Guy	Women want to sleep with Jerks

28

What all these mixed messages have done to you, the Nice Guy, is to give you really weird self-esteem issues. It impacts how you feel, not only about yourself as a Nice Guy, but also in how you see yourself in relation to the Jerk, as well as how you interact with women. On one hand you are happy you are a Nice Guy, but on the other hand, you also resent being a Nice Guy.

The Two Different Worlds for the Nice Guy

It is almost like there are two interchangeable worlds that exist for the Nice Guy, with two completely different sets of rules that exist for each of the separate worlds. In one world it seems like it is a great thing to be a Nice Guy. Then there is another world where it is a bad thing to be a Nice Guy. Now for the Nice Guy, these worlds go back and forth instantly, constantly, and without warning, (much like someone who has a split personality in the movies). What this constant and abrupt shifting back and forth between these two worlds has done is fill the Nice Guy with confusion and doubt.

Have you ever felt that confusion and doubt? Doesn't it feel like there are times when it is really okay to be a Nice Guy; when it seems like society rewards you as a Nice Guy. Not just with gifts, or thank yous, although those things are nice. This is about being rewarded with appreciation and respect. You feel content and relaxed around your male friends, and you even enjoy spending time with your female friends, socially. People like you and all is good. We will call that world, "the social world."

Now the other world is where it is not so good to be a Nice Guy, we will call that world, "the romantic world." You interact fine with your female friends, however when it comes to you trying to take your interactions to the next level, you feel limited and restricted. It is as if you are stuck on platonic island. When you try to go to the next level with her, that is when you try to turn things sexual or romantic, she will often respond to your advance with one of the many worn out clichés, which we have all heard before:

I see you as a brother

You are too important to me as a friend

29

Let's just be friends

I don't see you in that way

It's not you; it's me

I am not ready

It will make things awkward between us

You are not my type

You know me too well

You are just too nice

How Nice Guys Navigate the Social World

The social world consists of all the interactions Nice Guys have with people who are not sexual and/or romantic in nature. This includes your relationship with your coworkers, friends, family, acquaintances, and females in general. Now in the social world, it is great to be you as a Nice Guy. You care about people, they care about you, you are appreciated, you are relaxed, and you are at ease with who you are in your skin. You are comfortable and content with your niceness, and you feel appreciated for who you are as a person.

Most Nice Guys can navigate their social interactions reasonably well. They know the rules of social interactions for the most part and they are content where they stand socially. Most Nice Guys have friends or a social circle they spend time with and enjoy. However, when it comes to looking for and getting a girlfriend, romance, and/or sex, Nice Guys seem to trip all over their niceness. This brings us to the romantic world.

☢

How Nice Guys Navigate the Romantic World

Most Nice Guys already know about this world. This is the world where it is not so great to be a Nice Guy. In this world, you have much more difficulty navigating your interactions with women. You are constantly nervous, awkward, and insecure when it comes to women you are interested in.

You seem to have no problem being appreciated and recognized as a friend. But what frustrates you, is when women you are interested in consistently do not see you as "boyfriend material," or even a sexual option because of your niceness. Oh sure, they may even spend time with you, you may even go out with them and have a good time, but when it come to anything beyond that, you can forget about it.

Unfortunately, for you, it seems as if all of the traits that makes you a great social Nice Guy seem to make you a horrible romantic Nice Guy. It seems like all the caring and concern that you have for people in the social world does not work for the Nice Guy in the romantic one. It seems like the more you care, about the woman, the more concerned with her well-being you are, the more you are rejected.

All of these social, cultural, and media contradictions are put in place for one thing, and that is to keep you conflicted, confused, and filled with doubt. Because, when you are confused and filled with doubt, then you can be easily influenced. This makes it much easier for you to start to believe what the Conspiracy wants you to believe: that women do not want a Nice Guy, and/or that they only want Jerks. Furthermore, when you are confused, then it can also keep you from finding out who you truly are as a Nice Guy.

Who is the Nice Guy and Who is the Jerk?

A very important step in helping you (and Nice Guys like you) learn to use your Nice Guy tendencies to your advantage is by finding out who you are. If you do not know who you are, then it will be very difficult to figure what you want and/or need. First, we have to define who you are, and who is your competition. In other words, what exactly is a Nice Guy, and what exactly is a Jerk.

There is a major problem with rigid definitions, especially with words that are as subjective and as inflammatory as "Nice Guy" and "Jerk." The problem is that it is difficult for rigid definitions to take into account who you are as an individual, and your particular situation. Because of the Conspiracy, the average Nice Guy does not trust himself. When you do not trust yourself, the result is that you can lose yourself in the idea or ideal of what you think a Nice Guy is suppose to be. The very words,

"Nice Guy" automatically conjures up images in your mind of what a Nice Guy is and what he supposedly can and can't do.

When you are trying to figure who you are, a simple term like "Nice Guy" if you are not careful, can unintentionally restrict you. It can accidentally prejudice your ideas on who you think you are supposed to be, and how you think you are suppose to behave. You won't take the term Nice Guy and use it to serve who you are as a person, your wants, and desires. Instead, you will restrict yourself by letting yourself be defined by what you "think" a Nice Guy is suppose to be, or the stereotype of what you think a Nice Guy is. To complicate matters further, most Nice Guy definitions of what it means to be nice are dictated to them by the Conspiracy, which is working against the Nice Guy. For example, below are some of the many things people falsely believe.

Nice Guys:
Are only looking to be interested in long-term relationships
Are perfect
Don't get jealous, angry, or vindictive
Are only in monogamous relationships
Are boring
Don't yell, cuss, or get into arguments
Are not interested in casual sex
Are not suppose to experience negative emotions
Are not wild and crazy
Only put others wants and needs before his
Don't get jealous
Aren't interested in one night stands

The truth of the matter is that you already know what it means to be a Nice Guy, just like you know what it means to be a good friend. The true definition of what it means to be a Nice Guy, much like a good friend, is not stated in a dictionary, but in the deeds and the intent of that person. What it means to be a Nice Guy or a good friend is much larger than any explanation or definition of it.

If you have one hundred Nice Guys in a room, then you have one hundred different ways to be a Nice Guy. This book is less concerned with coming up with a standard definition of the Nice Guy, and more concerned with examining how the Nice Guy expresses himself and how effective he is. *Militant Nice Guy's* main concern is to help make Nice Guys more efficient and effective, not get lost in an academic discussion of what is and is not a Nice Guy.

Because of the extreme likelihood that you will be accidentally restricted by hard definitions in this instance, *Militant Nice Guy* takes the position that we should look at the definition of both the Nice Guy and the Jerk in much the same way we define beauty, porn, sexual harassment, and any other subjective term, you know it when you see it. Militant Nice Guy takes the approach that the best way for us to define who the Nice Guy and the Jerk are is to examine how both Nice Guys and Jerks respond to the same situations and examine their different viewpoints without fear or shame or the influence of the Conspiracy. This is for the purpose of helping you to determine for yourself what kind of Nice Guy you want to be.

☢

Who is the Jerk and Who the Competition

Now, in order to better help you understand who you are as a Nice Guy, we should first clear up a couple of misunderstandings. There is a lot of mislabeling going on when it comes to who Nice Guys refer to as Jerks. Nice Guys often wrongly label some guys as Jerks when they simply are not.

A significant reason why Nice Guys misidentify Jerks is because they are jealous or threatened of the other guy. Some Nice Guys will see a guy talking to, dating, or involved with a woman they want, so they automatically label him a Jerk simply because he is interacting or has a woman who the Nice Guy wants, or is interested in dating.

The Jerk is not necessarily someone who:
> Is better with women than you are
> Made a move first
> Is more charming than you
> Cooler than you

Has more resources or advantages than you
Funnier than you
You are threatened by
Has a bigger penis than you
Is richer than you
Is better looking than you
Got the girl
Is having sex/in a relationship with the woman you want
You are jealous of

Another problem a lot of Nice Guys have when it come to identifying the Jerk is that they often confuse the Jerk with the competition. Now you may be asking what is the competition, and how does he differ from the Jerk? The competition is the other viable option for her; he is the worthy opponent, another interested party, he could even be another Nice Guy. The biggest problem Nice Guys should really have with the competition is that they are simply in competition with them for the same women. For the most part, the competition, more often than not, are regular guys like yourself who probably have the same issues with Jerk that you do.

Valid reasons why women chose the competition over you:
Maybe he:

Had more charm	Dressed better than you
Had more money	Was better looking
Was her type	Had better chemistry with her
Was a better logistical fit	Was a better fit politically
Got there first	He expressed himself better

Most Nice Guys can deal intellectually and emotionally with losing a woman they want to superior or worthy competition. This is mainly because they know that her decision not to choose him is not based on him being "too nice," he may not like it, but he can understand it, make his peace with it, and move on. While is it disappointing to lose her to him, it is nowhere near as disappointing as being rejected for a Jerk who is obviously worse for her than is the Nice Guy.

Her poor choice would be understandable if she had no other options and she felt as if she had no choice but to choose him. It would make sense to us if she felt as if she could not do any better or if she was trapped financially, (maybe with a family or children), or some other logical reason.

If you are thirsty, would you drink a glass of water with dirt in it? You will if you are thirsty enough and the dirty glass of water is all you have. You may even be grateful for your dirty water because you know you have no other options, and dirty water can get the job done in satisfying your thirst. That makes sense to us, or it is at least understandable. What doesn't make sense would be for person to have a choice between a clean glass of water and a dirty glass and that person still chooses to drink from the dirty glass. This lack of understanding of that person's behavior is a very small example of the same feeling many Nice Guys have every time a woman chooses a Jerk over them. The following example illustrates this point.

I used to be really attracted to a woman named "Shelia." I used to go into this sandwich shop where she worked and flirt with Shelia all the time. Shelia once asked me why did I come into the shop all the time when the food was not that good? I said, "I come in here to see you." She told me, "I just met this other guy, I just wanted to be honest and let you know that there was someone else in the picture I was considering." I told her, "Thank you for your honesty." I still wanted to let her know that I still liked her, and I wanted her to consider me an option also. After she let me know where things stood with her and I let her know where I stood, we were now on the same page and it was good.

So I had fun with her for a while flirting back and forth, it was nice. We were getting closer, and then she told me how she had started see the other guy seriously, and how bad he was for her. I said, "What do you mean?" She said he was mean and controlling. I asked her, "Why did you choose to stay with him? Why didn't you leave him and get with me?" She said that she couldn't. I could not understand it, especially when she had another option in me that she could go to, but we still hung out.

We were getting closer and closer, and I could tell she was starting to get into me in a major way, but she was still with that Jerk. Then one day it had to happen. I had to ask her the question: the one I hate asking a woman. One I've asked too many times of women who are dating Jerks. I went into the shop, took one look at her face, looked her in her eyes, and I reluctantly asked, "Hey, where did that bruise come from?"

Now you already know the answer to that question. You know how the story goes, if it happened to her once, then it could happen again and it did. So after the fifth incident, I asked her, "Why in the hell won't you leave this guy and be with me? It is obvious that he won't stop beating you?" I figured that me not beating her would be reason enough, but sadly it was not. She said she could not be with me because she was committed to him. Now here is the funny part, she later broke up with him to get with another guy who also hit her.

Her not choosing me did make me wonder, *What is so bad about me that she would rather be beat by a Jerk than to be with me?* I may not have been the best looking guy, or the funniest, or the smoothest, but I was not a complete asshole to her, and I did have her best interest at heart. I wish I could tell you how much that incident affected me, or how it left some deep psychological scar on me. I want to say this is what started my journey to understanding Nice Guys, but it did not.

The sad thing is that I am not even revealing something personal about myself. For something to be personal, it has to be unique to you. Unfortunately, this is not a unique experience for me, this and similar stories have happened with Nice Guys all over the world. I just figured that since women's rejections of Nice Guys for Jerks was so common, I just assumed that this was just how things were suppose to be for Nice Guys. I thought women just preferred Jerks to Nice Guys no matter what, even Jerks who beat their women. I now know that it does not have to be this way anymore for the Nice Guy, especially when you understand what it means to be a Jerk.

In short, Jerks for the most part are selfish, that is they are primarily interested in their own gratification. Now everyone is interested in their own gratification, or their own happiness, there is nothing wrong with this fact. This thinking only turns to someone being a Jerk when the guy goes about trying to get what he wants at the expense of another person with whom he is interacting.

This examination of what it means to be a Jerk is meant to put us on the same page so that as Nice Guys, we have a better idea of what we are up against. You have now taken a necessary step in combating the Jerk by getting a clearer picture of who he is and what he wants. Now that you have a clearer idea of what it means to be a Jerk, let us now turn our attention to what it means to be a Nice Guy.

Misunderstanding What It Means to be a Nice Guy

Now, before helping you understand what it means to be a Nice Guy, we have to clear up a major misunderstanding about what that term actually means. For so long, the Conspiracy has force-fed the idea that Nice Guys are romantically inferior and we automatically accept it as part of what it means to be a Nice Guy. This damages how we see ourselves.

If you want to see evidence of how the Conspiracy has damaged the Nice Guy's self-esteem, then ask the average Nice Guy why he thinks he is unsuccessful with women. A surprising answer you will often get is because he thinks he is too nice. I know this because I have asked this question to groups of Nice Guys (as well as individual Nice Guys) hundreds of times. Every time I hear that phrase "too nice," I ask, "What does that mean? How is it that you lose a woman or can't get a woman because you are too nice? How can someone be too nice, explain that to me, please?"

After I ask that question, I usually get some variation of one of the following phrases:

I get nervous around women

I do not trust myself

I do not know what to say to her

I do not have any confidence in myself

I was not sexual enough for her

I get uncool around her

I let women run over me

I am too needy

I do not know what to do around women

I am too boring

These "so-called" Nice Guy traits are often used to describe Nice Guys because so many Nice Guys have them. What is unfortunate, is that most people do not even realize that these traits have very little to do with what it means to be a Nice Guy. These traits are only the signs of a Nice Guy who has been manipulated to believe that he is not worthy of successful interactions with women.

Believing that neediness, lacking sex appeal, or lack of confidence etc., is a natural part of being a Nice Guy is the same thing as believing a sore throat and a runny nose is a natural part of being a football player. Those in the know understand that those traits are not traits of a football player. Instead, they are the traits of a football player who has something wrong with him, or is sick. It is the same with the Nice Guy, except instead of him being infected with the cold or the flu; the Nice Guy is infected with low self-esteem.

The difference between the Nice Guy and the football player in this case is that the football player knows something is wrong with him and will take steps to address his particular situation. The Nice Guy will often think things are suppose to be this way and just accept his condition. He will accept his second-class status because he believes this is what it means to be a Nice Guy.

Many Jerks (and women) also believe these unfavorable traits are what it means to be a Nice Guy. A major mistake the Nice Guy makes when discovering and defining what it means to be a Nice Guy for himself, is not realizing that they do not have to automatically accept these unfavorable traits that the Conspiracy has infected into us.

Realizing that you do not have to accept these unfavorable traits is that first step to either rejecting them outright, or analyzing them to try to learn from them. Because you now know that these undesirable traits are not normal for the Nice Guy, you now know that if you experience them, then it means something may need to be addressed.

CHAPTER THREE

CARING AND HOW IT HELPS TO DEFINE THE NICE GUY

The Nice Guy Disadvantage

If you want to be a more efficient Nice Guy, then you have to know and understand your inherent disadvantage when it comes to interacting with women. You must also understand the Jerk's inherent advantage when it comes to getting and keeping women. The one trait that makes you such a great social Nice Guy is also what makes you such an ineffective romantic Nice Guy. Ineffective means in terms of getting and keeping women. The same trait that makes Jerks so bad for women in the long run is the very same one that makes him perfect at getting women, keeping women, and for stealing women from you.

This trait is caring. This is the single most important and defining characteristic of the Nice Guy, and his caring is what separates him from the Jerk. Caring is the source of much frustration for many Nice Guys. This is because it seems to many Nice Guys that the more you care about the woman, the more your ability to get and keep the woman diminishes.

The reason you will always be at a disadvantage when it comes to interacting with women and defending yourself against the Jerk is simply because you care about her. Caring and how we deal with our caring is the core issue in the battle between the Nice Guy and the Jerk. Why do Jerks seem to get the women they do not care about? Why does a Nice Guy have such a hard time getting and keeping the woman who he cares about? That is what we will examine in this section.

To help you to better understand how caring works for the Nice Guy, *Militant Nice Guy* has broken up the concept of how the Nice Guy cares into two sections: the conceptual, and the practical.

With conceptual caring, we will focus on why and how you care, and what that means for you emotionally. We will look at how the Conspiracy has turned your caring against you by distorting and misrepresenting what it actually means for the Nice Guy when he cares.

The practical section will focus on your actions and how you behave because you care, and how your caring manifests itself practically and tangibility. This section will focus on examining your interactions and how you act and react as a result of the Conspiracy's manipulation of you.

The reason why we are making the two distinctions is because the Conspiracy has combined them to confuse the Nice Guy. If he is confused about how he cares, then he will have no control over it. He will feel as if he is ruled by his desires, instead of him being able to enjoy his desires. His lack of control will eventually lead to the Nice Guy becoming ineffective at communicating, and as a result, dissatisfied with himself.

The Nice Guy may even get to the point where he resents the fact that he cares so much. He hates that he cares because his caring is often a source of pain for him. It hurts to care about someone and for them not to care about you, or to see them run off with some Jerk who does not care about her as much as you do. When he starts to resent how he feels, then it will be easy for him to start resenting himself. This is why we have chosen to divide caring up so you can see how one side influences the other, and vise versa.

How the Nice Guy Cares PART 1:

What happens to Nice Guys who care?

Now, what does it mean when you care about someone? Simply put, it means you are emotionally invested in that person. An emotional investment is much like a financial investment. When you are financially invested in a business, your happiness or well-being is in some part tied to how well the business is doing. It is perfectly natural to be concerned with what is happening to the business in which you are invested. Naturally, the more invested you are in the business, the more concerned you are with how the business is doing.

It is the same thing with a romantic investment. Your happiness in part is tied to her well-being and how she is doing. As a result, you want to make sure she is okay; you do not anything to happen to her, nor do you want to do anything to her. Furthermore, you are sensitive to how she feels, and you try to be aware of her wants and needs. Your actions and responses are based in part on how you think they will affect her. This is mainly why you are at a disadvantage when it comes to the Jerk, because he does not care.

It would benefit Nice Guys greatly by understanding that caring is not a disadvantage; it does not make them weak. They are at a disadvantage because caring makes them inefficient especially when compared to the Jerk who he is in competition with. If Nice Guys learn how to start caring about women more efficiently, then they will be in a much better position to interact with the woman, and defend themselves against the Jerk.

Recognizing you are at a disadvantage as a Nice Guy is not necessarily a bad thing at all; it is not a reflection on you as a person, it is just a characteristic of being a Nice Guy. The term "disadvantage," when used is this context is simply meant strategically, and not as a character flaw. You care about her well-being, and there is nothing wrong with that as long as you know what kind of position that places you in when it comes to interacting with her. Your caring gives you boundaries that you as a Nice Guy will not cross. The Jerk has no such boundaries.

Some of the traits you develop when you care about someone may include:

Being considerate of what they are going through

Trying to be respectful of their feelings

Being loyal to them

Being fair (you do not want to take advantage of them)

Being reliable (you want them to know they can depend on you)

Trying to be understanding

Being giving

Being compassionate

Being forgiving of their mistakes

Over investment (Caring too much)

Caring is the cause for many issues for the Nice Guy when it come to him interacting with women. It's not necessarily just because he cares, but because he often cares too much. This caring too much is what will often cause him to be over invested in his interactions. This has a tremendous influence on how much he is attached to the outcome of his interaction or interactions with a woman. Over investment occurs when you are invested in something to the point where it is no longer productive or healthy for you to continue.

☢

Some examples of where you may be over-invested in a woman:

Most of your decisions concerning her are based on fear

You spend more time worrying than you do enjoying her and/or the interaction

You are overly concerned with what she may be thinking

You are afraid to walk away from her

You fear you can't be yourself around her

You spend a majority of the relationship/interaction waiting for your investment to pay off

A major problem many Nice Guys have with caring is that they often let their caring get the better of them. This means they get wrapped up in their caring and their emotional investments, and they let them overwhelm them. As a result of caring too much, the Nice Guy will often lose his perspective when it comes to interacting with women. The emotional investment he gives to the woman is/will be disproportional to what she gives him and/or where the interaction is at that time.

Because his investment is disproportionate to hers, this will often cause the Nice Guy and the woman who has his interest, not to be on the same page. He cares to the point where he places extreme value and importance on every little thing she says, does, and thinks. As a result, he often develops a hypersensitivity to everything she does. Every little action she takes becomes a monumental event of huge importance in his eyes.

Instances of where over-investment can affect a Nice Guys' perception of a woman's actions include:

Doesn't call him right back (Over invested Nice Guys may take this as a rejection/avoidance of him)

Casually touches him during conversation (He may take that as her showing romantic interest in him)

Doesn't laugh at one of his jokes (He may take that to mean some thing is wrong ,or she doesn't like him anymore)

See her interacting with another guy (He thinks, *Oh no, this guy is a threat and I need to handle him.*)

Asks can he buy her a drink and she accepts (He takes this to mean he now has a good chance at sex with her)

Now this is not to say that those interpretations are not possible or likely. The problem with being over invested or caring too much is that it becomes harder and harder to judge your interactions accurately the more invested you are. This is because the more invested you are the more danger you are in of losing your perspective.

The Not-Caring Approach

The Conspiracy has manipulated many Nice Guys into believing the best way for you to deal with over investing is to not to care at all, or to care as little as possible. I am not a fan of the not-caring approach because much of the joy and pleasure in life comes from caring. What we care about helps to define us and gives our lives and relationships meaning. I often wonder how those who advocate the not-caring approach find pleasure and enjoyment with the women with whom they interact, if they do not care about them?

The reason why the Conspiracy advocates the "not caring" approach is because when it comes to interacting with women, it can work. "Not-caring" works for the Jerk, but the Conspiracy never tells the Nice Guy why the "not-caring" approach works for the Jerk, and not for him. It works for the Jerk because it is much easier to manipulate and control someone when you do not care about them.

Using someone to get what you want is called objectification. For the purposes of this section, when you objectify someone, you think of someone as a means to an end. You primarily see them as what they represent to you. A means is something you use to get to what you really want. Let's try some examples, with different professions: bank tellers, mailmen, and bartenders.

Now these folks may be people, but they are important to you primarily because of what they represent to you, and not who they are as people. They are representatives of your money, your mail, and your drinks. Now most people are familiar with and/or have people like this in their life. These people are only relevant to you in so much as what they can do for you. They have little relevance to you as people in and of themselves.

Most people don't even know their banker tellers, mailmen, or bartenders' names. Some do, some may even be fond of these people, or have some type of personal relationship with them; however, that relationship more than likely is based on what that person can do for you. You do not interact with them independently of what they can do for you. Furthermore, if these people stopped doing whatever they were doing for you, then your interactions/relationship with them would more than likely end, or at least be greatly reduced. This is where the Jerks excel when it comes to getting, keeping, and controlling women. Jerks primarily see women as a means to an end; as a result they do not have to deal with or at least are much less affected by emotional consequences. Consequences one will have to deal with when they hurt or use someone they pretend to care about.

This is why it is difficult to make the not-caring approach work for the Nice Guys, because not-caring works best when you have no emotional attachments to the person or the outcome. Nice Guys by their very nature care. This frustrates Nice Guys because they see the things Jerks have done to women, and have not only gotten away with them, but were often rewarded for it. The Nice Guy is frustrated because he feels restricted by his caring, he often may start to see his caring as a weakness. This is because he believes that he cannot do the things he see the Jerk doing and get the results he sees the Jerk getting from women.

So why care if it makes you less efficient in getting what you want? Why do it, especially if not caring about a woman often makes it easier to get what you want from her? Here is a little secret for you. Even if you do get what you wanted from the woman because you did not care about her, or because you manipulated her or played her, you will rarely be fully satisfied or fully enjoy your success. A big reason why you won't enjoy your success is because there was little or no emotional investment in the person. As a result, your victory or success in getting what wanted is hollow. Without a genuine investment in what you are doing with that woman, your interactions are reduced to an execution of moves devoid of passion, instead of an emotional dance between the two of you.

Pleasure and enjoyment are both enhanced by caring about what happens. If you do not care about anything that you are doing, then you will have very little meaning and/or joy in what you are doing. I am sure you have seen this with people who have jobs they don't particularly care about. It's not necessarily that they hate their jobs, it's just that many times they do not have any strong feelings one way or the other about their work. What often happens is that one day just kind of bleeds into another, and they find themselves living for the weekend. At least if you hate your job, then you have some kind of feeling about it. Often those who hate their jobs will use their hatred of their job as motivation to find another one. If you do not care, then you will have no passion. Passion comes from caring.

There is no man alive who will ever forget his first car. It does not matter if his car was brand new fresh off the car lot, or if it was a piece of crap you had to push to start. It was your first car and you will never forget it. Now most men can barely remember their third car, and if they do, then their memories of that car have nowhere near the same emotional impact as their first car.

Why is that? Most people's third car is vastly more superior in every way shape or form to their first car, so why does the first car hold so much more meaning to him? Men feel this way because their first car had the most emotional impact on them, because that was the car they cared the most about.

Why is the average male more emotionally invested in their first car instead of their third? A man is more emotionally invested in his first car because to the average man it represents to him his first real taste of freedom and responsibility. No other car he has owned since the first can ever duplicate that feeling. Although his first car was probably technically inferior in every measurable way shape and form, he cares about it more than the others because his first car had the biggest emotional impact on him. His caring is what gives his first car that special place in his heart. It's not what you care about, it's just that you care. We give value to people and things that make an emotional impact on us, and as a result, those things help to give our lives some meaning.

One of the reasons why people have a hard time getting motivated is because they do not care about what is happening. They are not interested in what is going on and they have a hard time getting motivated to invest themselves or to take action. I find it very interesting that often when I am out with guys in a social setting, especially at bar or a club, one of the guys will usually say something to the effect: "I can't believe there aren't any women here, let's leave." This will often be said even when there are a significant number of women around. It took me a while to understand what these guys were really saying. The issue is not a lack of women, but a lack of women there who they are interested in meeting, or that they care about.

Another reason why you should care is because in the long run it is worth it. For example, take a woman who is considering sex with one of two guys. Her requirement for sex with her is that the guy has to be in an exclusive relationship with her after they have sex. Now, because the Jerk doesn't care, and is only interested in sex, he will say whatever she wants him to say in order to get what he wants from her.

The Nice Guy will not. This is because he cares about himself and her. He wants to get her with integrity. Sure he could use her to masturbate like the Jerk, but the Nice Guy knows that he would be cheating himself because he was not true to himself. Part of what makes sex with women good is a mutual connection, a sensitivity to the other person. This is a major benefit of caring about the other person, it will deepen your interactions and relationships.

This is a major reason why *Militant Nice Guy* rejects the not-caring approach because Nice Guys are not unfeeling, uncaring robots. When you care about someone, it is very difficult to stop your true feelings from coming out. When you try to hide how you feel then your feelings will often come out some other way. You might as well own how you feel so you can have some kind of control over it.

How Nice Guys care PART 2:
Attachment to Outcome

It is extremely difficult to communicate effectively if you listen to those who say you have to hide your feelings, and that caring about a woman makes you soft, less of a man, weak, etc. There seems to be a major prejudice against caring and being attached to outcome. The Conspiracy treats your desire to have an interaction go well as if it is a bad thing. Caring about how your interactions go is not a bad thing. It is totally understandable and natural to want to have an interaction go well with a woman, especially someone to whom you have an attraction.

You have been trained to doubt and question your desires, wants, and needs. This brainwashing is why many men think they need to turn their back on their caring, wants, desires, and attachment to outcomes. Now when the Conspiracy tells you not to care, they may not say it as blatant as this, still, they are telling you to hide how you feel albeit in a much more subtle way. A few of the many ways you may have heard this sentiment expressed is:

Make sure she cares about you more than you care about her

Always lead the conversation

Control the woman

You should be cold and unfeeling

Dominate the interaction

Don't show her your emotions

Be an alpha male

Always be closing

Don't show weakness

Always stay positive

Never trust a woman

Have an abundance mentality

All of these phrases can best be summed up under the idea of being free from your attachment to the outcome, and/or your outcome dependency. Attachment to outcome is when you have some degree of investment or interest in the outcome of a particular interaction. In other words, this is where you care about and hope your interactions with women go well. The Conspiracy has been pretty successful in making Nice Guys fear attachment to outcome.

Now the reason why we are examining attachment to outcome is because it is the practical tangible part of how the Nice Guys cares. In this section, we will examine the results of what happens to Nice Guys who are over invested or care too much. And we will look at how the Nice Guy behaves/responds as a result of him being over invested in the outcome.

Why Nice Guys Should Not Let Go of their Attachments

Many Nice Guys believe that freedom from attachment to outcome is the right way to go. This is why many Nice Guys try the not-caring approach when it comes to dealing with women.

The not-caring approach is attractive to Nice Guys for three main reasons:

1. Because the Nice Guys' current interactions with women are ineffective or unsuccessful. As a result, he is in the perfect position to be open to trying something new. He feels he has nothing to lose.

2. Because he is jealous. The Nice Guy sees the Jerk getting anything and everything he wants from women and he wants that for himself. He often wonders to himself, *Why am I doing all of this and getting nothing? The Jerk does not care about her and gets every thing he wants.*

3. Freedom from pain. The Nice Guy feels he can lessen the pain of rejection by not caring about the interaction. If the interaction goes bad, or if she rejects him, then he won't hurt too badly. He can act as if he never cared about what happened in the first place.

Those reasons coupled with the Conspiracy brainwashing, has caused many Nice Guys to try the, "freedom from attachment" approach. This often comes in the form of them trying to get the girl, or what they want from her, by trying to act as if they do not want her or care about her. They believe this method works in part because they see the women they are interested in falling all over Jerks who obviously do not care about them. As a matter of fact, it appears too many Nice Guys, the more disinterested the Jerk acts, the more she wants him. The Nice Guy knows the Jerk does not care about women as much as he does. Therefore, he thinks there may be some merit in the not caring approach. The Nice Guy thinks that is how he needs to be to succeed. So he tries to be like the Jerk and act cool, aloof, and disinterested and it often does not work out too well for him.

This is because being cool and aloof only works for people who are actually cool and aloof. Too many Nice Guys try to hide what they are feeling for numerous reasons. The main reason we will focus on right now is because they do not believe in how they feel and who they are. They do not trust themselves enough to be able to put their real selves out there and get what they want, so they try to use the technique of being cool and aloof in order to get her. In other words, to get the woman they want, they believe they have to try to pretend as if they do not want the woman.

What is ironic about this is the fact that you are trying to pretend as if you do not care about her, which only means you really do care about the outcome of the interaction. If you really did not care about how the interaction went, then you would not have to focus on not being free from your outcome. Also, if you were truly not attached to outcome, then you would not feel disappointed when your interaction did not go the way you wanted it to go. Trying to hide how you feel and what you want is not a productive way to go about getting what you want. All you are doing is setting yourself up for likely disappointment.

Trying to hide how you really feel is off-putting to people because many times people can pick up on when someone is not being genuine. They may not be able to tell exactly what it is, or be able to articulate it, but they can tell that something is off (especially women). This is a big part of the reason why Nice Guys can come off creepy and weird to women. That is because when you care about the outcome and try to act like you don't, then you are being inconsistent. People can pick up on your inconsistency, even unconsciously. They can tell you are not being genuine and/or something is off. This is a significant reason why you do not succeed when you try to act like the Jerk or try to come across as uncaring.

Why You Should Care About Outcome

The reason the Conspiracy wants you to be free from outcome is to dilute your purpose and destroy your focus. When you do not have a focus or goal, then you will not know what you want, as a result, you will not have any standards by which to judge your interactions. You will not know how to gauge what is happening and/or how well things are going. You will not know where to take the interaction. The best example of this is when Nice Guys say they do not know what to say to a woman they are interested in meeting or approaching in general. A common reason for this feeling is because they know they want her, but they do not know why. This is because if he knew why he wanted to talk to her, then this knowledge would give him a clue of what he would want to say to her.

When it comes to talking to women, your attachment to outcome is what guides you; it is the reason you are talking to her in the first place. The Conspiracy will tell you to just be in the moment, and to just go up to her and talk to her and to let the conversation flow. If that was the case, then the generic advice on how to initiate a conversation with a woman: "just go up to her say hi and just be yourself," would have worked for you by now. But if you have a goal when talking to her, say, getting her number, trying to ask her out for coffee, or simply just getting to know her better, then you would have something to focus the conversation on besides just talking to her.

The Conspiracy tells you if you are not attached to outcome, then you can never lose, you will always succeed. For example, let's say you are following the Conspiracy's advice when it comes to having an interaction with a woman you just met, which is just letting the conversation flow freely. Now what if as a result of the conversation, she decides to give you her phone number? The Conspiracy would have you believe that you should see her deciding to give you her number as a bonus. Now, if you were talking to her and she did not give you her number, then it was no big deal because you did not want it in the first place. This is because you expected nothing and just went with the flow or did not care.

Well this line of thought is only productive if you did not want the number in the first place. This would be fine if you were just talking to her just for the simple pleasure of talking to her. However, what do you do if you were into her, and did want her phone number? According to the Conspiracy, I guess you could act like you did not want the phone number in the first place because wanting the number shows an attachment to outcome. The very nature of freedom from outcome does not allow you to be proactive in going after what you want. It is no wonder the Conspiracy uses this method to neutralize Nice Guys.

The very nature of freedom from attachment, or just being in the moment without purpose, means that you are just reacting to that particular moment in time. As a result, you are at the mercy of whatever the moment has in store for you. This is not an indictment of freedom from attraction because there are many times when some people do just want to live in the moment and be free from outcome. It's okay to just have a conversation or interaction just for the sake or pleasure of doing so.

The issue *Militant Nice Guy* takes with the freedom from outcome approach is that it is not a practical method when you have a desire, an interest, or expectation for an interaction to turn out a certain way. Another problem with freedom from attachment is that Nice Guys are not being fair to themselves. That is because they often do not want to use freedom from attachment as it was really intended, which is being open to whatever the moment decides to give you. They want to experience all the joys of success of an interaction when it goes well, but none of the disappointment of when an interaction goes poorly. Part of being open to what the moment gives you is accepting the fact that you have four likely outcomes: Sometimes something good will happen; sometimes something unexpected will happen; nothing will happen; or something bad will happen. When it comes to going after what you want, disappointment is often is as much of a possibility as is happiness. The only sure way to not to experience disappointment is not to play the game.

How Much Are You Invested in the Outcome?

Most Nice Guys see themselves as either attached or not. They think their attachment is like a light switch that is either off or on. Instead of seeing attachments as either or, I invite you to try another approach, you may want to try seeing your outcome dependency as a gauge that measures how attached you are to your outcomes. Once you know how attached or invested you are, or how much you care about the outcome, then you will have a clearer picture of how to proceed.

If you know the level of your investment in the outcome, then you will have a much better idea of where you stand and how much you are attached or interested in your outcomes. This knowledge will go a long way to helping you to conceive, calibrate, and execute an appropriate response for your particular situation. The reason why this is a more productive option for you is because this allows you to enjoy the interaction without you becoming obsessed over it.

When you keep track of how much you have invested, then you put yourself in a much better position to be able to have a proportional response/reaction to the outcome. The best way to have a proportional reaction/response to a situation is to properly invest in any situation based on the stimuli received. In other words, do not take on more than you can handle emotionally, and learn to keep things in proper perspective.

Perfect examples of keeping your emotions and actions in proportion to your situations, are blackjack tables and slot machines at casinos. Each blackjack table has what is known as table limits. There is a minimum you can bet and there is a maximum you can bet, and each table has a different minimum and maximum amount you can bet. This is the same with the slot machines, there are slot machines that start at a penny per pull and some machines that go up to whatever dollar amount you want to gamble.

Casinos do this in part so that you can have the full gambling experience that is proportional to your level financially. The thrill or enjoyment of the gambling experience comes from risk and tension. The more you invest or risk, the greater the intensity of the experience, the highs are higher, and the lows are lower. In order to have the full gambling experience safely, you need to know some very important things about yourself, probably the most important of which is knowing what your financial sweet spot is.

You can best reach your sweet spot in this instance by knowing how much money you have to risk. If you risk too little, then you will not care about the outcome. You will either be a little numb to the experience or you will, more than likely, just end up going through the motions because you do not care. If you risk too much, then you will be too attached or over invested in the outcome, and your emotions will end up controlling you.

In order to have a proportionate response in your interactions, you have to know three things: who you are, what you want, and how that relates to your environment. This is important so you know how much to invest in your interactions. The same way it is important for gamblers to know their financial status, and the table/slot machines limits, Nice Guys need to know their mental status so that they will know how much to invest when they are interacting with someone.

Many people mistakenly believe we suffer because of our attachments, this is not entirely the case. It is not necessary our attachments and our caring that causes our suffering, but many times our disproportionate response to the situation that is usually the problem because we are over invested. This is because we often let our emotions overwhelm us and this is usually the reason why we responded disproportionately. This is because we did not channel or express our emotions relative to the situation we were in and we let our emotions control us.

For example, my friend was at a bar talking to a woman, and she asked him to buy her a drink. His response to her was, "Do you think I am stupid enough to buy a woman I just met a drink? What kind of fool do you take me for?" Now I know what he was trying to do, he and other friends of his have been taken advantage of in the past by women who like to use men for free drinks. He was trying to keep that from happening to him again. He was trying to protect himself from being taken advantage of. His head was in the right place, it was just that his response was not proportionate to his situation, and he let his very valid fear overwhelm him. He could have simply told her something to the effect, "I would love to, but how do I know you are not one of those girls who uses guys for free drinks?" This would have gotten the same point across without being as intense.

If you do what Conspiracy wants, and believe that we should be free of attachment and free from outcome, then you believe we should reject a big part of what allows us to have full and authentic experiences in life. To act like we do not care about something that we care about is not natural. This is why it is such a struggle for the Nice Guy to let go of his attachments because our attachments are a part of who we are, and it is hard to deny who we are, and what we want.

Trying to act like you do not care about an interaction going well when you are invested in it is like trying to act like you don't care about a significant amount of money you bet at the blackjack table. If you truly did not care, then you would not be trying to act like you don't care about it. The fact that you made a bet/talked to her, makes you invested in the outcome. The only question is: are you in control of the investment or is the investment in control of you?

Why Goals, Markers, and Principles Are Important

Having goals, markers, and principles in place is the key to monitoring how invested you are in your outcome, and keeping things in perspective. I believe this is the best way you for you to enjoy your attachments while keeping them in perspective. This way it will be harder for them to overwhelm you, or for you to lose yourself in them. Having goals, markers, and principles in place will help you to define what you want, and what you will do to get it. They are important because they help to define who you are as a person, and they help to give you direction and purpose. Goals, markers, and principles can also guide you on your path to help you to get what you want.

Goals

Our goals are what we are trying to accomplish. They are what motivates us and gives us purpose and direction. Goals can be as big wanting as to be governor, to as simple as wanting to walk up to attractive women and flirt with them. It does not matter what your goals are, or even if you express them out loud. What matters is that you have them; your goals are primarily for you. Our goals go a very long way to influencing and defining who we are.

If you know someday you want to be governor, then that choice will guide and influence everything in your life. From what schools you choose to attend, your choice of major, to the types of jobs you choose to take, to the types of people you want to be around. If you know the type of women you are attracted to and why you are attracted to them, then that knowledge will affect how you will proceed. From where you go to meet them, to what you will say to them, to how you will interact with them.

When you do not have any goals, or when you do not know what you want, then you may feel a little lost and kind of like you are drifting. That is because when you have goals and know what you want, then you feel inspired. You are inspired because you have purpose. When you know what you want, that knowledge will help you both directly and indirectly put together a plan of action on how to achieve that goal. That plan that you put together is an important part of defining what you want because it is your path or your road map to your goal and/or purpose.

Think back to all the times you were having a conversation with a woman you were interested in, but you felt like the conversations was going nowhere. The conversations were pleasant enough, but you often felt as if the conversations were directionless and/or had no sense of purpose. This is often the best sign you had no goals or you did not know what you wanted from her before you started talking to her.

Another prime indicator of having no purpose in you interaction is after you are done talking to her, you are left feeling neutral, not good or bad, just neutral. The conversation probably ended with some variation of: "So, uh, yea, I guess I'll talk to you later." You are not even sure how to feel about the conversation: *Did it go well? Did it go bad?* A major reason why you are not sure where you stand exactly is because you had no goals for the conversation; you had nothing in place to work toward, or judge yourself or the conversation by before you started talking to her.

Because you did not know what it is you are trying to accomplish with the woman, you do not know how to measure your progress during the conversation. Knowing what you want and having a standard to judge the conversation by will provide the basis for how you will go about improving your interaction the next time around, because you will have a purpose for talking to her.

Now imagine if you were talking to a woman and you had a goal in mind let's say you wanted to get her phone number. Now you have some place to take the interaction. You would naturally be more efficient and effective because your interaction now had a purpose and a reason for happening. Even if you did not succeed in getting her phone number, you would now have a standard to judge your interaction by. Also, because you have a standard, you can use it to help you to improve and do better the next time you talk to a woman.

A major reason why you have conversations that do not go anywhere is because you had no idea where you wanted the conversation to go. Too many Nice Guys just want to keep the conversation going with a woman because they think that is what they're supposed to do. A Nice Guy thinks he is making progress by having idle conversation with a woman . He makes his main goal to talk to her instead of focusing on what he wants from the conversation.

☢

Markers

Our markers are how we keep track or our progress while we are in pursuit of our goals. They are like the mile markers on the side of the highway, letting you know how far you have traveled, and how far you have to go to your destination. Markers can also let us know how much we have invested in our outcomes.

For example, if you wanted to be governor, then markers in this case might be that while on the road to becoming governor, first you have to graduate from high school and college; hold elected office for at least one term; get financing, put together the right support team, and so forth. When it comes to flirting with women, a marker may be that you will flirt with a woman; but if she is not smiling within five minutes of you talking to her, then you will leave or, adjust your conversation accordingly.

When you have no way of measuring your progress, then you are in danger of giving up on your goals because you have no way to know if you are progressing or not, or where you stand in relation to achieving your goals.

☢

Principles

Our principles are our boundaries and limits that also define in part who we are. Principles are what give shape and form to our goals and ideals. Principles are our own personal belief system, or code of conduct.

Your principles are so you won't lose sight of who you are while you are in pursuit of your goals. Principles tell you that even though you want to be governor, you will not lie to the voters to get elected. Or your principles may be that you may want to flirt with women, but she has to be over twenty-one. Our principles are what help us to maintain our integrity.

When you do not have any principles, then you do not have any integrity. There is nothing you won't do to get what you want. When you do not have any integrity, as far as having a line that you will not cross, then it will be all too easy for you to say or do anything in order for you to get what you want, especially when it comes to women.

If you have no principles, then all of your decisions and value will be filtered through the prism of the result. This is a case of the ends justifying the means. This is how most people lose themselves in a woman, or in their attachments, and become wrapped up in their goal of getting her at any cost. If you do not have any principles, then you will do anything to get her, everything is an option; lying, cheating, manipulation, threats, anything.

Other examples of goals, markers, and principles:

Goal: To have one million dollars saved in the bank
Marker: To save $100,000 a year
Principle: Will not do anything illegal to get the one million

Goal: To go on more dates
Marker: Have to ask two women out a week
Principle: She has to be Catholic

Goal: To lose 25 pounds by the end of the year
Marker: Weight myself every two days
Principle: Will not take diet pills

Goal: To get a job
Marker: Must go on three job interviews a week.
Principle: Will not take any job that involves lying or manipulation

Having goals, markers, and principles are a major key to being a more effective Nice Guy and expressing yourself more efficiently. In order to express yourself efficiently, you have to at least know what you want, where you currently stand, and a direction of where you want to go. Most Nice Guys who do not have goals, markers, or principles just kind of wander along and let things happen to them. This is not an indictment against not having goals or a purpose, there is nothing wrong with that as long as it is done by choice.

This book is not saying that every interaction needs to have some kind of goal to them or lead to something. Sometimes, the goal is just the interaction itself. There is nothing wrong with enjoying interacting with someone just to do it, if that is your desire.

For example, imagine you are wandering on a beach during your vacation. You do not have any goals or a destination because you are just enjoying the scenery. It is impossible for you to be disappointed because disappointment comes from having unmet expectations, and when you are wandering you have none. Wandering the beach was the point.

There is nothing wrong with wandering the beach in and of itself. However, there is something wrong with wandering the beach and finding yourself disappointed because you did not end up someplace exciting. This is because you were expecting something more from aimless wandering than what it was meant to give you. Many times Nice Guys do not want to wander without a sense of purpose, they want to have influence and control over their environment. Having goals, markers, and principles is one of the best ways for the Nice Guy to enjoy his interactions without getting lost or losing himself in them.

CHAPTER FOUR

WEAPONS OF THE CONSPIRACY

This section is devoted to some of the weapons the Conspiracy uses on Nice Guys like you to keep you full of doubt and shame, and, as a result, under control. This section will examine the lies, misinformation, false promises, and half-truths used against the Nice Guy to make him think something is wrong with him for being a Nice Guy. Let's star this section off with examining negative emotions.

Negative Emotions and the Nice Guy

Many Nice Guys are frustrated with being a Nice Guy in part because they see and experience not only constant rejection from women, but women picking obviously inferior Jerks over them. Because of this frustration, many Nice Guys may start to develop some qualities to deal with their constant frustration in interacting with women ineffectively.

Some of these qualities include:

Defensiveness	Timidity
Doubtfulness	Anxiousness
Controlling	Neediness
Pessimism	Fearfulness

These are examples of negative thoughts. These negative thoughts are a reflection of how someone may feel about an involvement in an activity that they believe will not result in a good outcome. Let's take for example you approaching or interacting with women. You develop a negative thought or attitude when you believe that the activity you are about to take part in will go poorly, or you believe that you do not have the ability to favorably influence the interaction in which you are about to partake.

These negative thoughts often manifest themselves when Nice Guys are confronted with a situation that reminds them of a time when they have tried and failed before. Because these negative thoughts make the Nice Guy feel bad, he will seek to avoid any situations where those feeling come up, and, as stated earlier, that is how the Conspiracy beats you.

Negative emotions are the natural results of how the Nice Guy feels about his inability to favorably influence their interactions.

Examples of negative emotions Nice Guys feel:

Shyness	Anxiety
Neediness	Depression
Self-hatred	Confusion
Sadness	Anger
Frustration	Disappointment

Fear of negative emotions can adversely affect Nice Guys' interactions with women. Because of fear of their negative emotions Nice Guys will be reluctant to:

Approach women in different settings

Go out to meet women

Take a woman on a date

Move on and get a new girlfriend

Tell her how much he likes her

Say what he really wants to say

Ask her for her phone number

Talk to women confidently

Ask a woman for sex

If you do not do any of these things because of your fear of negative emotions then someone else will. Someone who is not afraid of their negative emotions, and knows how to use them will show up and take the woman you are interested in dating. And, more than likely, that someone is the Jerk. This is a major part of the Conspiracy's plan to control and neutralize you, by making you fear your negative emotions. If you fear something, then you will always be ruled by that fear, and make the same mistakes over and over again. Fear of negative emotions makes Nice Guys' behavior predictable to the Jerk. If you never talk to women because you are afraid of your negative emotions, then the Jerk has won. He does not ever have to worry about you interfering with him when he is interacting with women. He wants you to be afraid of negative emotions because he knows that you will forfeit all the women to them. Because you are afraid, you will not go after what you want.

How I Discovered the Power of Negative Emotions

Around the time I started interviewing Jerks about why they were so successful with women, I simultaneously started to take a hard look at not just my lack of progress and standing with women as a Nice Guy, but other Nice Guys as well. I have spent over twenty years making self-help/improvement my passion and trying to be not only the best Nice Guy I could be, but a positive Nice Guy as well. After my personal difficulties, and witnessing other Nice Guys' difficulties in dealing with women, and not succeeding. I was forced to accept the evidence. Either there was something wrong with positive thinking or positive thinking was not enough. Nice Guys are generally considered to be more positive than Jerks, yet they are consistently losing women to Jerks who are often considered anything but positive. I wondered why this seemed to be the case.

I've had several conversations with different Nice Guys over the years about how their women left them and/or rejected them for a Jerk. virtually all of the conversations had the same theme. It was some variation of: "I do not understand how she could leave me or reject me for someone who is so clearly not good for her. What is wrong with me? I am a Nice Guy… a positive guy. Why doesn't she want me?"

Jerks stealing women from positive Nice Guys would not be a problem if it were just happening to me…or just a random Nice Guy. This would be easily understandable if this were the case, because that would mean that these were isolated incidents. But Nice Guys have been losing women to Jerks all over the place, universally, the same way. I do not think this is just a coincidence. This is a major part of what motivated me to start to investigate negative emotions, and examine how they relate to the Nice Guy.

After examining all of the evidence, I was forced to accept that there were many lessons the Nice Guy could learn by listening to his negative emotions instead of automatically fearing/ignoring/rejecting them. I believe the Conspiracy makes the Nice Guy fear his negative emotions unnecessarily so that he can never learn how to properly channel or use them.

Fanatical Positive Thinking

Now to be crystal clear, *Militant Nice Guy* is not against positive thinking and positive thinkers. *Militant Nice Guy* is against fanatical positive thinking and fanatical positive thinkers. Fanatical positive thinking and thinkers were put here by the Conspiracy to make sure the Nice Guy fears the negative side of himself. Fanatical positive thinking sees no value in negative thoughts, emotions, or feelings, and subscribes to an obsessively positive lifestyle where negative thinking has no place.

Examples of fanatical positive thinking:

Automatically sees negative emotions thoughts and feeling as bad things

Believes positive thinking is the answer for every problem

Equates seeing the benefit of negative thoughts with being anti-positive

Believes having negative thoughts means there is something wrong with you

Believes positive thinking alone is a an acceptable plan of action

Believes no good can come from examining your negative emotions

Negative emotions are like the negative side of a car battery. The negative side of a car battery is not seen as bad, in fact without the negative side of the battery working in harmony with the positive side, the car would not run. Having negative emotions, thoughts, or feelings does not automatically make them bad for you. What determines whether an emotion is good or bad for you is how you respond to it.

Why You Fear Your Negative Emotions

I believe the Nice Guy would benefit from learning to understand his negative emotions, and learn to use them for his own benefit. There are those of you who may ask, "Wouldn't learning how to use and listen to my negative emotions make me a more negative person?" Anyone who asks those very legitimate questions is seeing negative emotions the wrong way. They think negative emotions in and of themselves are bad. We are examining our negative emotions to make you a better Nice Guy, not to make you a so-called "negative" person.

We automatically fear our negative emotions because we don't understand them, most Nice Guys have no other relationship with their negative emotions other fear, shame, and loathing. Too many Nice Guys have been wrongly trained to think that just by experiencing, thinking, pondering, etc., negative emotions are automatically bad; or they think having these negative thoughts makes them a bad person. You may think negative emotions such as anger, depression, and sadness are automatically bad things. You may even think something is wrong with you for even having negative emotions. This is not necessarily true.

Here is an example of not listening to your negative emotions: A friend of mind was working out with some friends when he felt a sharp pain in his leg. He wanted to stop working out and tend to it, but his friends told him to stop being negative, and push through it. They wanted him to ignore information that his body was giving him…that something may be wrong with him. However, they saw it as him making an excuse, and that he was not being positive. As a result of listening to his friends, he decided to ignore this "negative" information for two weeks.

After the pain got too severe to ignore any longer, he went to see the doctor, and he was surprised to find out that he had damaged the muscle in his leg and had to have surgery. The doctor told him the treatment would have been a lot simpler if he would have come to him sooner, and asked him why he waited so long to deal with it. My friend told the doctor he wanted to, "tough it out," and "be positive." It is the same with your negative emotions, if you do not listen to them, or choose to ignore them, then not only could you be missing valuable information to help you, but you could be making things worse for yourself in the long run by not listening to them.

It is a common misconception to think your negative emotions will eat at you and destroy you, you are told this so you will fear your negative emotions. What will eat at you and destroy you are not your negative emotions, but not expressing your negative emotions properly. If you do not take some time to listen to your negative emotions, then you are in danger of having your emotions grow unchecked, and that is how they will blind you and consume you. Healthy expression of your negative emotions is the best way to properly channel your negative emotions for your own good.

How Your Negative Emotions Give You Your Integrity

The number one problem with living the fanatical positive lifestyle is that it is fundamentally a lifestyle of no integrity. Fanatical positive thinkers like to change the rules to benefit themselves. While there are benefits to being positive, fanatical positive thinking allows you the ability to twist and distort situations and outcomes to have them mean anything you want to mean, instead of seeing things how they really are. This is the very nature of fanatical positive thinking.

I was at a men's self-improvement meeting and one of the members there "Chris" was talking about how he was having a hard time attracting Mexican women to date. Chris felt as if there was some reason Mexican women did not like him. He was t rying to work his way through this issue, by trying to figure out what he could do to better attract them. Unfortunately for Chris, there were a lot of fanatical positive thinkers there and they proceeded to tell him that he was being negative and that he should just focus on being positive. They suggested he change how he thinks.

"Marcus," who was one of these fanatical positive people was at the meeting and asked him if he had met every Mexican woman on the planet? Obviously Chris's answer was no. Marcus said, "If you have not met every Mexican woman on the planet, then how can you know if what you are feeling is true?" He told him he was suffering from limiting beliefs and that he needed to believe in himself more and just believe that Mexican women are attracted to him. Everyone in the group agreed he should be more positive and started to come up with way for him to remove his negative thinking.

As a little experiment I decided, to ask Chris what types of women were attracted to him. He said Black women. No one at the meeting had any problems whatsoever with this answer. No one wanted him to change his thinking. How come no one ask him the same questions he was asked before? How does he know that all Black women are attracted to him? Has he met every Black woman on the planet? The same thought processes he used to come to the conclusion Black women love him is the same thought process he used to come to the conclusion Mexican women hate him.

The reason no one had a problem with his answer is because his point of view in this case matched their "positive" point of view. They did not even stop and examine his thinking to see if his "positive" thinking was justified or accurate. It was just outright accepted because they liked his answer, just because it was a so-called "positive" one. Instead of examining his perceptions to see if they had any merit, or to see if there were any lessons to be learned, they wanted to ignore what he was feeling because it was inconvenient.

If you do not question your thought process when it gives you a "positive" thought that you like, then you cannot turn around and abandon that same thought process when it gives you a "negative" thought you do not like. If you do this, then you rob yourself of your integrity.

Fanatical positive thinkers are fair-weather friends, they only want to accept when you are positive, but they have no place for you if they perceive you as being negative. This is because fanatical positive thinkers are frightened by doubts and questions. They live in a perfect "Utopia" where nothing bad is suppose to happen. They don't like questions because the philosophy of fanatical positive thinking means there is no room for doubts or questions. As a result, fanatical positive thinkers are constantly changing what they want to believe. How can you ever truly trust yourself if you are constantly changing what you believe, depending on what situation or circumstances you are experiencing?

Jerks and Their Negative Emotions

Doesn't it seem like the worse Jerks treat women, the more they love them for it? Why do women constantly run from the Nice Guy over and over again when he has nothing but positive emotions and intentions pouring out of him toward the woman he is interested in? Why does it seem as if women always runs into the arms of some Jerk who cares about her much less than the Nice Guy does. Ironically, the Jerk often makes no secret of this fact. In some cases, it even appears as if the Jerk flaunts his negativity and/or negative behavior and she still runs to him.

Examples of negative behavior Jerks get away with:

Disrespect	Mean-spiritedness	Emotional abuse
Arrogance	Insulting behavior	Physical abuse
Doing things she doesn't like		Rudeness
Inconsiderateness		

Nice Guys have seen the Jerk consistently rewarded for his disrespect, for his unreliability, for his rudeness, for his dishonesty, and the like. But what reward does the average Nice Guy get for being good to a woman? If he is lucky…he gets nothing. If he is not so lucky, then his reward will be to watch her run off with some Jerk, leaving him to be by himself, wondering what he did wrong. Let's look at how the Jerk is rewarded for his negativity.

Examples of how Jerks are rewarded for their disrespect of women

They are rewarded with a woman's:

Time	Money
Sex	Loyalty
Relationships	Caring
Appreciation	Love

Many Nice Guys are shocked and stunned not only by how women seem to be drawn to Jerks' negative behavior, but how in many case women don't even seem to see their "negative" behavior as a bad thing. Often, for reasons that will be explored later in the book, women will misread or interpret the Jerks negativity as something positive.

Examples of how women misinterpret Jerks' negative behavior

When the Jerk is being stubborn	She sees him as being strong
When the Jerk is being insulting	She sees him as funny

When the Jerk is being possessive	She sees him as knowing what he wants
When the Jerk is taking her for granted	She sees him needing her
When he is not there for her	She sees him as busy/focused on his goals
When he is just being horny	She sees just passion

The following is a perfect example of a Jerk being rewarded for his negativity: "Stephanie," a female coworker of mine had gained some weight. She was self-conscious about it, and was trying to lose it. Most of the guys who worked with her were encouraging of her, positive, and supportive of her efforts to lose her weight, all but "Brian," the Jerk.

He actually mocked all of the guys who were being positive in support of Stephanie. His thinking was, "being nice" is no way to get her. He said the best way to get a woman is to prey on her insecurities. To prove his point, this is what he said to her, "You know I used to think that you were really sexy before you got fat. Back then I thought about asking you out but, not anymore. Tell you what, I'm going out of town for two months, if you lose the weight by the time I get back, then I will take you out and we will have a good time."

We were all shocked when we heard him tell her this. Now here is the funny part, while Brian was gone out of town she went to the gym and lost the weight and used Brian's promise to take her out as motivation. All of the other guys there who were giving her positive encouragement did not seem to motivate her to lose the weight. All the positivity surrounding her did not matter to her, the only thing that mattered to her was Brian and his negative comments about her weight.

The fact that Brian insulted her and called her fat did not matter. The fact that he was preying on her insecurity about her weight did not matter. I asked her, "Why do you want to lose the weight to go out with someone who insults you?" Her response was, "If I lose the weight and he takes me out then I know I'm good enough to be with him."

Nice Guys were falsely led to believe women would not respond to Jerks' negativity. However, Nice Guys know this is not true because they see women constantly reject the positive Nice Guy for the negative Jerk, over and over again. The question most Nice Guys have in regards to the Jerks, "How do you stop the Jerk?" The best way to fight him is to realize that you cannot stop him. It is a mistake for Nice Guys to think in terms of stopping the Jerk. Once you realize that you cannot ever completely stop him, then you will be in a much better place to deal with him.

Nice Guys have been fooled into thinking they can stop the Jerk and are disappointed when they cannot. You have been told you can stop the Jerk so that you will waste your time focusing your attention on him. The Conspiracy wants you to focus on him so that you will not focus on improving yourself and understanding who you are. We cannot ever completely control what someone else will do. The only thing we really have control over is ourselves. Before you can effectively fight against these Jerks, you have to understand who you are. In order to understand yourself, you have to have an honest, unbiased assessment of yourself. It is hard to do this if you ignore a large part of what you are thinking and feeling, in other words, your negative emotions.

How Negative Emotions Keep You From Deluding Yourself

There is a very popular expression which says, "There is no such thing as failure, only feedback." If you want to have a life full of authentic experiences, then you have no choice but to accept that the reverse of this saying is also true: "There is no such thing as success, only feedback." For some reason ,the reverse of this expression is rarely heard. Why is that? Because, if you were to accept the reverse expression, the fanatical positive thinkers would lose their hold over you. They'd lose their hold over you because you would be forced to accept that there is much more to life than just positive thinking. Fanatical positive thinking is delusional thinking because its very nature keeps you from seeing the whole picture.

When you delude yourself, you live in your own reality. You see things how you want to them to be, and not how they really are. For example, the homeless guy arguing with the imaginary person who is not really there. The weird guy in the club who thinks everyone wants him. How about the guy who weighs three hundred pounds and thinks everyone thinks he looks good in spandex? Even the kid who talks to his imaginary friend. Delusions big or small keep us from interacting effectively in our environment. This is what ignoring our negative emotions can do to us.

An important question many people want the answer to is how can you tell for yourself when you are having a delusion, or, if you are seeing things accurately? The problem with defining delusions is the same standards you use to show you are having a delusion, are the same standards you would use to show a normal processed belief. With this problem in mind, a good guideline would be to look at how you deal with the possibility that you might be wrong in your thinking/belief when you are confronted.

Do you automatically dismiss the thought that you are wrong without examination, or do you examine the possibility? If you do immediately dismiss the idea you may be wrong, then the question is why are you being dismissive? Are you dismissive because you have proof your belief is correct, or, do you immediately dismiss the possibility because you are threatened by the thought of you being wrong? These are very important questions, which only you can answer for yourself.

Fanatical positive thinkers often automatically dismiss contradictory thoughts, views, and questions because this information is a threat to their world, and not necessarily because they have proof that their thinking is correct. If the person in question doesn't have some type of answer to the question, "Why do you believe what you believe, or how did you come to that conclusion?" If this person does not have some type of proof or justification for thinking the way they do, then they may suffer from delusional thinking.

Examples of delusional thinking:

Constantly seeing/spinning situations so only you benefit or come out looking good.

Instantly seeing others with different opinions than yours as inferior or bad people.

Giving yourself much more credit and/or blame than you deserve. For example, positive thinking will make my illness go away.

Automatically thinking your way is the only way, or taking the "my way or the highway" mentality.

Refusing to see people or situations how they really are instead of how you want them to be.

You are immediately dismissive of any comments, criticisms, or advice that does not paint you and/or your actions in a favorable light.

You believe you do not make mistakes.

Three major problems with deluding yourself:

1. It will be difficult for you to able to trust yourself.
2. Others will not trust your opinions.
3. You will have a hard time learning from your mistakes.

This example helps to show how we delude ourselves with only being positive and ignoring negative emotions: A few years ago I was having a debate with a friend "Jimmy." We were debating the best way to handle a woman's rejection. What started this debate was we were at a happy hour with one of his friends, "Andy." Andy was upset because a woman he was trying to pick-up had rejected him. Andy asked his friend Jimmy for advice on how to deal with the rejection. Jimmy told him, "When a woman rejects you, it does not matter, and it is not important." He went on to say, "When a woman rejects you, you should not take it personally, how could you, she does not know you, so you should not let her rejection bother you. You should just take the rejection and put it out of your head."

Something about his advice bothered me. I asked him, "If you believe that we should not take rejection personally, then how should we deal with acceptance?" What prompted me to ask him this question was because I remember two months earlier I was hanging out with these same guys. Everything was the same, Jimmy and Andy at the same happy hour, and we had the same scenario except with a different woman. Andy went up to a woman with the same approach, but this time she accepted his advance and he got her phone number. Jimmy told Andy he should be proud of himself for getting her number, for being a real man, for going after and getting what he wanted.

I asked, "How you can say that rejection does not matter, and that he should not take it personally? Just two months earlier you told him in the same scenario that, 'You should be proud for going after what you want.' How can one situation be any more valid than the other because one situation had an outcome you did not like, and the other one did? You are deluding yourself with positivity to keep from feeling the pain of rejection." You know what he told me? He told me I was being negative. I did not know how to articulate my feelings at that time, but what I now realize is that if you want a life free of delusion, then you have to accept all outcomes, not just the positive ones. This part of living a life of integrity.

If he wanted to dismiss the rejection because of some valid reason: she was married, in town for the one day, not interested, didn't speak English, or whatever, then fine. However, if he rejects a scenario out of fear or because he did not want to feel bad, then there is an issue. See, when Jimmy said rejection did not matter, his statement was not based on truth, it was a delusion based on reluctance. Most Nice Guys are reluctant to deal with rejection because they cannot handle it. Therefore, what he tried to do was pretend as if rejection does not matter; he was deluding himself.

Deluding oneself is often easier than accepting reality. The Conspiracy knows part of having an authentic experience is sometimes having to accept a certain level of doubt and uncertainty at times. Fanatical positive thinking can free you from doubt and uncertainty, but the cost for this freedom from doubt is often delusion.

The problem is that rejection does matter to you. If rejection did not matter then you would not dwell on it so much. For you to act like rejection doesn't matter is not productive or healthy for you. More importantly, you are lying to yourself, and it takes a lot of energy for you to lie to yourself. The more you try to ignore something, or lie to yourself about it, the more energy you give it. This is why rejection eats at you because you refuse to deal with it, or express your feelings of rejection in a more productive way. Instead of trying to bury your rejection with a delusion, why not learn what your negative emotions are trying to tell you.

Your negative emotions can help you to put things in perspective so you can understand and learn from your experiences. When it comes to rejection, the best way to put it in perspective is to find out why you were rejected. Too many Nice Guys see constant rejection as automatic proof that they are not good enough to interact with a woman. Many do not even think to examine the rejection to see if there is anything to learn from their rejection. There are many lessons Nice Guys miss because they do not examine their rejections.

Examples of lessons you can learn from examining your rejections:
> If it was something you did wrong in that situation
> Whether you should take your rejections personally
> If there are some personal issues you have to deal with
> How to possibly not make the same mistake again
> If there is some issue she is dealing with
> What you did right

How Listening To Your Negative Emotions Can Help You

To use your negative thoughts, emotions, and feelings in a productive way, you have to have an understanding of where your negative emotions come from. When you understand where your negative emotions come from, then you will be in much better place to deal with them. Just as I said that you should not be blinded by positive emotions, the same holds true for negative emotions.

Clearly analyzing and trying to make sense of your world is almost impossible to do when you do not listen to and/or are afraid of your negative emotions. We have been so well trained by the Conspiracy to instantly hate all things negative. Although, there is valuable information for us to learn from our negative emotions.

For example, let's take a look at the word hate. There are many people who say you should never hate. I still find it hard to believe there are actually people in the world who believe no good can come from hating someone or something. My former coworker was a sweet old lady; she used to think the same thing. She looked like your gray-haired grandmother, and we used to call her, "Granny." Well, whenever I was at work talking about how much I hated someone or something, she would pinch me on the arm in that way only a grandmother can and sternly tell me that I should never hate. She even hated when I would just say the word hate.

Her logic was that hate was a negative emotion, and no good can come from being so negative, or "don't be such a downer," she would always say to me. I said, "What if someone hurt you physically or emotionally to the point where you felt justified in your hatred of them. Would it be okay to hate then? Is that reasonable?" She said, "No, you should just let it go."

I have often heard her and people like her who believe the same thing. She believes the reason you should never hate someone or something is because whatever you hate is like a cancer that will eat at you until it destroys you, and you will never get over it. They say you can't keep your heart full of hate or you will never be able to move on, and you will never be able to get over your pain.

Well with all due respect to "Granny" and everyone who agrees with her, I believe they are misinformed. A lot of good and productive things can come from hating something or someone. I am living proof of that.

Let's look at some of things I have hated in my past:

I hated being fat

I hated not making enough money

I hated watching my friend's son get bullied at school

I hated how much of a procrastinator I was

I hated not telling off my boss for how bad he made me feel

I hated that I never followed through on writing my book

Now the funny thing is that I have always felt fine and content with myself, even with all of this so-called hatred that I supposedly have hidden deep inside me, eating at me, and destroying my soul. The question is: How can I be so content with myself and feel fine? This is the exact opposite of what Granny, and people like her, say. They contend that my hatred is bad and that it will destroy me. The reason why my hatred has not eaten at me or destroyed me is because I've learned not to fear my hatred. I listened to it instead, and channeled it in a productive way.

When I started to listen to and accept what my hatred was telling me without fear and prejudice, then I slowly started to figure out what I had to do. My vision started to become clearer because I now started to see what I had to do in those particular instances. My hatred gave me a sense of focus and purpose, and it gave the clues to me, discovering what I had to do for myself.

When I listened to what my hatred was telling me, I then learned:

I had to go on a diet

I needed to get a new job

I had to give him my advice on how to handle this particular bully

I had to focus on getting things done

I had to tell my boss what he did to make me feel bad

I sat down and wrote what is in your hand

I later learned that my hatred was good for me in many of those instances. However my hatred was only good for me because I was able to channel it effectively. You can use any emotion, either positive or negative emotions in a productive way if you are not afraid to listen to what they have to tell you. After you learn to listen to what your negative emotions are telling you, then you can actually start to learn to use them for yourself.

It's not the hatred itself that destroys you, it's the lack of making peace with the hatred that destroys you. Believe it or not, most people hate something in their life: child abusers, racist, Nazis, men who abuse women, mean people etc. These people have no problem with their hatred fundamentally, and society at large has no problem with these people hating who they hate. Why? Because most people have made their peace with their hatred in these instances.

Implementing/Using Your Negative Emotions

I believe examining and processing your negative emotions can give you important clues to help you figure out what to do in different situations you may encounter. The following story illustrates this point perfectly.

A dating coach friend of mine, "Michael," was telling me about a problem he was having with one of his students, "Adrian." Michael told me Adrian had no problem approaching and talking to women at the mall, bookstores, coffeehouses, on the street anywhere. As a matter of fact, he was excellent at it. However, Adrian's problem was that he was terrified of approaching and talking to women he would see in a nightclub.

I asked Michael why his was student so afraid to talk to women in the club. He said whatever his reason was did not matter because it was all in his head. He thought addressing Adrian's negative thoughts only served to magnify his negative emotions. He thought his negative emotions needed to be left in the past, and he should just live in the moment. Michael felt that as soon as he could get his student into a positive mindset and state, then his problems would go away.

I asked Michael if he would have a problem with me talking to his student and surprisingly, he said, "Go ahead." I asked his student why he was so scared of talking to women in the club. Adrian said, "I am scared that if I were to go up to a woman and say the wrong thing that the woman would get pissed and would throw a drink on me and I would be embarrassed."

I asked him to tell me his story of why he was afraid. He told me he was in a nightclub a long time ago and he was talking to a woman. He thought she was attractive and he loved the dress she had on and wanted to tell her so. He told her he thought the outfit she had on was flattering. I said, "What was wrong with that?" He said, "She thought I said that her outfit was fattening, and she threw a drink on me."

I smiled, and I told him, that I had a similar experience. In my case the woman who poured the drink on me thought I was someone else. I walked up to her to introduce myself and out of the blue, boom, red drink all over my white shirt. When she saw who I was, she tried to apologize; she said that she thought I was someone else. That did not matter, what mattered was everyone had seen an attractive woman pour a drink on a "creep." Why was I a creep? Because I had a drink poured on me by an attractive woman. Everyone automatically concluded I must have done something wrong and I deserved to have her pour her drink all over me, all because she was attractive.

It's amazing how small things like that can affect you. As a result, I used to have a severe reluctance to talk to any woman holding a drink in her hand. Furthermore, what this incident proved to me was that if something were to go wrong during an interaction between a man and an attractive woman that most people will side with the woman automatically, even if she was at fault. Adrian felt the same way and incidents like these and many others make us and many Nice Guys like us feel like we have to be perfect when interacting with women, especially if they are attractive.

Adrian asked what I did to get over my fear of that happening again? I told him my initial solution was simple. Whenever I went out, I would always keep an extra shirt in my car. I've done this for years now, and I have not had that issue since. We laughed at how simple the solution was. He tried it and he has not had a problem since talking to women in the club because of the drink issue

My fear was not necessarily of me having a drink poured on me, my fear was me not having a response to having a drink poured on me. I feared not being prepared, and having an extra shirt in my car was a bad-ass response in my mind. The reason why the solution to our problems seemed so simple is because we listened to what our negative thoughts were trying to tell us. I did not try to have him push through them, ignore them, or demonize them.

If I would have been only positive, and just ignored my negative feelings then I would have been ignoring not only the lessons from my past, but also ignoring part of myself. My fear and Michael's student's fear were based on some event that happened to us in our past. These events made an impression on us; our fear or our negative emotions did not just come out of the blue.

Most Nice Guy's fears have a basis in something, and to ignore that experience or trying to bury it with positive thinking is nonproductive. The reason why the dating coach's advice was having a hard time getting through to his student is because he was not acknowledging how his student was feeling, he was being dismissive of his experience.

Another Example of Implementation of Negative Emotions

Let's take a guy who is afraid of approaching and talking to women he is attracted to, or one who does not like speaking in front of people because the thought of it puts him "on edge", or give him "butterflies" in his stomach. Now, if he just did nothing about this "negative" feeling then he would not learn why he had this feeling.

One reason why he may have butterflies is because he is nervous. Most people think being nervous is a bad thing because they do not know exactly what being nervous means. As far as these particular situations are concerned, he is nervous because he hopes his interactions will go well. If you want something to go well, then that means you are usually ready to execute your plan, and you want your plan to work. In the case of talking to the woman, that could mean that he wants her to like what he has to say. Or, in the case of talking to groups, he hopes the audience will like his speech. The main issue in these two cases is execution of his plan. That would be him knowing/ believing in what he wants to say and saying it and waiting for the result.

Another reason he may have butterflies is because he is experiencing anxiety. Anxiety is completely different from being nervous. People often confuse the two. People experience nervousness when they want something good to happen. People experience anxiety, that they think something bad is going to happen. If the guy in the example is experiencing anxiety, then more than likely it is because he thinks something bad is going to happen. If he thought something good was going to happen, then he would not be experiencing anxiety, he would be nervous. However, most guys feel so bad about having anxiety until they never take the time to examine what their anxiety means or to see if it is even warranted.

Maybe he is experiencing anxiety because he thinks his interactions with the woman will go poorly because he doesn't know what to say or he thinks that she will not believe what he has to say to her. A possible solution for this issue could be for the guy, to say exactly what is on your mind. For example, "I think you are attractive and I wanted to say hi to you, just go easy on me, because I am really nervous. I don't normally do things like this."

If he thinks his interaction and speech is not going to work out for him, then it would benefit him to find out why he feels or thinks this way, instead of instantly dismissing his thought as negative thinking. Maybe he thinks that the audience will not like or judge what he has to say. You are only afraid to be judged if you believe the ruling will not be in your favor. If this is his feeling, then a possible answer for the guy could be that his speech is not ready and needs more work.

Now I am not even remotely trying to suggest that by listening to your negative emotions, they will give you solutions to your problems that quickly or at all. But I am sure your negative emotions do provide the clues to how you can go about solving your problems.

CHAPTER FIVE

THE CONFIDENCE MYTH

You have to have confidence to get women.

This statement/belief is arguably the most dangerous weapon used by the Conspiracy against the Nice Guy to make him ineffective with women. If you were to ask any woman what she wants in a man, I am willing to bet confidence that will be somewhere at the top of the list. When Nice Guys ask for advice on how to be more successful with woman, they will often hear some variation on the phrase, "Women like a confident man." As a matter of fact, confidence seems to be the magic bullet answer for all of the Nice Guy so-called problems with women.

I don't know what to say to a woman?
Have confidence.

How can I get her to like me?
Just be confident.

Why did she leave me?
Because you were not confident enough.

How can I get her phone number?
Ask for it confidently.

Why won't she have sex with me?
Women sleep with confident men.

Women say they love a confident man, and because of this, Nice Guys want confidence and believe that if they can get confidence then their problems with women will magically be solved. The Conspiracy has caused many Nice Guys to believe they cannot get and/or interact with a woman effectively without confidence. But the funny part is you are

78

never told exactly what confidence is. If you do not know what confidence means and/or what it feels like to have confidence, then how do you know when you truly have it? The Conspiracy has taken the term confidence and has expanded, distorted, and abused its definition to the point where it means something different to everyone to the point where it has almost lost all of its practical value.

What is Confidence?

Confidence is simply a measure of your competence. If you have high confidence in yourself, then you believe the chances you will succeed in whatever activity you are about to take part in are high. If you have low confidence in yourself, then you believe that the chances of you succeeding in your activity will be low. If you are preparing to take a test and you have studied for the test and know the material backwards and forwards, then you will have high confidence that you will succeed in passing the test. If you did not study for the test, then you will have low confidence that you will succeed. You cannot just manufacture confidence out of the blue to help you with your test. Confidence does not work that way.

Just Have Confidence

"Just have confidence," is what many self-help gurus, women, and even Nice Guys tell other Nice Guys when it comes to dealing not only with women, but life in general. The problem is that when you want to know how to proceed, the "just have confidence" advice has little practical value for you when it comes to execution.

Hypothetically, if a Nice Guy, let's say, "José", came to me for advice on the best way to ask out his coworker, and I told him to ask her out confidently, that advice would be of no practical value. When most people give this advice, it is usually a sign that they have nothing of practical use to offer. If I knew of something practical to help him, some piece of practical advice, which he could place his confidence in then that would be much better for him.

For example, let's say I knew that they both shared the same favorite author, and he was in town giving a sold-out seminar, which I knew she wanted to attend, I also knew José had two tickets to it. How do you think he would feel about asking her out then? He would naturally have more confidence in asking her out. This confidence would not be the baseless confidence that the Conspiracy advocates, but confidence that is based on something practical. It is based on the fact that he has high confidence that she will go with him because he has tickets to an event she wants to go to.

When women say they want a confident man, what they are really saying is that they want someone who has the self-assuredness, which comes with someone who has belief in their abilities. He has this self-assuredness because he believes he will succeed in whatever endeavor he is about to partake. You can only get this type of confidence when you have confidence in something real. When José, now armed with this new knowledge, decides to ask out his coworker, he will naturally be more at ease and more self-assured because he has high confidence that he will succeed in getting a yes from her. His confidence is based on him having the tickets to an event she is interested in attending.

Sure you can have baseless confidence, but that is not confidence, that is faith. The thing with baseless confidence is that sometimes people do get what they want when they put their belief in this baseless confidence. People will often use this success as proof of the effectiveness of the, "just have confidence" theory.

☢

However, there are two problems with this type of confidence.

ONE: *You can't learn or grow from it, or improve upon it. If this confidence is not based on anything other than something that you pulled out of the air, then how can you rely on it? You do not know how your confidence works or how to manipulate it, because it is beyond your control.*

Let's say José asked out his coworker with baseless confidence and she said yes. The ironic thing is that her saying yes to going out with him was based in large part on his confidence, that is him knowing what he wants and what he is doing. But the problem is his confidence was not based on anything concrete. As a result, it will be difficult for him to have direction and purpose over his future interactions with her because his initial interaction with her is primarily based on confidence, which he pretended to have. He will be at a loss with what to say to her, what to do with her, or how to be around her overall. How can he know how to proceed if his confidence is not based on anything but faith?

TWO: *If people fall for your false confidence, then you will have to deal with the pressure of being called out on your confidence, or having your confidence tested. You will then have to stop acting confident and start being competent, or risk being revealed as an imposter.*

Acting or just being confident it is not productive for the Nice Guy in the long run. This is because he is pretending, lying and/or bluffing about having confidence. Because of this, he will constantly live in fear of the truth being found out. Even if he is never discovered he will know the truth, which is his confidence is based on a lie or him pretending. Bottom line: it is not based on anything of substance.

I remember when I met a particular imposter who was pretending to be the drummer for a famous rock and roll band. He was able to fool people because the band wore make-up and costumes on stage and no one knew what they really looked like when they were not on stage. All he had to do was act the part, or act confidently, and he had everyone, including me, fooled. He stayed at the finest hotels, ate at the best restaurants, and spent time with some amazing women all on the strength of his confidence. But when it came time for him to prove who he was and play the drums, his scam fell apart, and he was discovered…and went to jail.

Genuine confidence is earned, and part of earning confidence is knowing why you have confidence and what you have confidence in.

Nice Guy Confidence vs. Jerk Confidence

Anyone who believes that Nice Guy's difficulty with women comes from a lack of confidence, does not understand what it means to be a Nice Guy. A vast majority of the Nice Guy's difficulty with women does not come because the Nice Guy does not have any confidence, it comes because the Nice Guy has integrity. A major concern the Nice Guy has is how will his behavior affect the woman he is interacting with? This is not to say that he is not interested in pleasing himself, it is just that he is also concerned about what effect his actions will have on her well-being. Because the Nice Guy is concerned for her well-being, he will often hesitate to take action.

Nice Guys understand that a woman's emotions are not to be played with or taken lightly. This is especially true of someone who they care about and/or are interested in meeting. Because of this, he will often be hesitant in his actions. Nice Guys hesitate out of respect for the woman, and because they have integrity. They hesitate not because they are weak, or because they lack confidence. They hesitate because they are considerate. Ironically, this hesitation is what causes many people, especially women to wrongly believe the Nice Guy has no confidence.

Part of caring about how your actions affect someone, means that you will have to accept a certain level of uncertainty when dealing with them. This is in part because you are not a mind reader, and often you will not know the best way to proceed to do right by her. To make matters worse, a vast majority of Nice Guys, women, and others, will often misinterpret this appreciation and consideration of her in many different ways, which are nonproductive for them. Many will see the Nice Guy's behavior and Nice Guys themselves as:

Weak

Indecisive

Unsure of himself

Scared

Beta

Unworthy

Unconfident

Most Nice Guys have had the unpleasant experience of having a Jerk steal a woman from them. What often happens is while the Nice Guy is "hesitating," trying to decide how to best proceed, some insincere Jerk slides in and takes her from him. It is almost as if the Nice Guy is being penalized for his respect and decency. The Jerk does not care about being genuine, he'll lie, manipulate, imply, do or say anything, to get her because his number one priority is to himself. This is what the Jerk is doing, while the Nice Guy is trying to be considerate, and trying to figure out how best to precede without disrespecting or hurting the woman.

The Jerk does not have any of the concerns and caring that the Nice Guy has exhibited. In fact, his lack of caring is a plus for him when it comes to getting what he wants from her. It is ironic, because of the fact that the Jerk does not care about her, means that he is in a much better position to be able to say and do things with or to her, which the Nice Guy is reluctant to do out of fear of hurting her.

This is what many people, especially women, mistake for the confidence that all Jerks are suppose to have. It is not that the Jerks are more confident than Nice Guys, it is just that the Jerks simply do not care, and women wrongly see the Jerks lack of caring and integrity toward them as confidence.

Being genuine is one of the traits that separates the Nice Guy from the Jerk. Jerks are concerned about saying and doing anything to get her; while Nice Guys are concerned about being genuine while trying to get her. The Jerks' lack of concern about the effect his actions has on her frees him from worrying about what she thinks. As a result, this gives him a sense of purpose and laser-like focus that most Nice Guys can only dream of having. Nice Guys see the Jerk rewarded for their lack of integrity and Nice Guys feel trapped by their integrity.

☢

The following is an example how Nice Guys are trapped by their integrity:

I once had two coworkers, "Jason" and "Scott;" both had tickets to a football game. Now "Trish," who was also our coworker, was a football fanatic. Both Jason and Scott knew this about her and wanted to ask Trish to the game, but they both knew Trish had a major exam the next day.

Jason wanted to ask her to the game, but he knew that she was going to be busy studying because she had a test on Monday, and the game was on Sunday, the day before the test. When he did decide to ask her out, he was not as insistent as he could have been because he was taking her wants and need into consideration. I heard him ask her to the game and this is what he said, "Hey, I know you have to study this weekend, but do you think it would be possible for you to come to the game with me?" She told him, "No thanks, I appreciate it, but I have to study." Jason said, "I understand. Good luck on your test Monday."

Scott also wanted to ask her out, knowing the same thing Jason knew, but the difference is that he did not care about her or what was going on in her life. I heard him ask her out to the game. He said, "Hey, I want you to come to the game with me." She said, "No thanks. I appreciate it, but I have to study." He said, "I don't care, I want you to come to the game with me." She said, "But this is a really important test." He said, "I don't care. I want you to come to the game with me." She said, "OK".

After she left, I asked Scott why he insisted on asking her out when he knew that she had an important test on Monday. He told me "I am going to tell you like I told her, I don't care. I told him, "You are such a Jerk, He told me, "You know what else I am? Busy on Sunday with Trish." Later, when I asked Trish why she chose Scott over Jason, she told me, "Scott just seemed more confident to me, like he knew what he wanted, he just did not take no for an answer."

This is an excellent example of why the Nice Guy appears to lack confidence when it comes to interacting with women, especially compared to the Jerk. The Nice Guy cares about the outcome, and cares about the woman he is interacting with, therefore, he is less self-assured about his influence on the outcome than the Jerk. This is because he is concerned about more than satisfying himself. He is also concerned about satisfying her. The Jerk naturally has more confidence, or is perceived to have more confidence than the Nice Guy because his self-assuredness comes from knowing what he wants from the outcome without the burden/consideration of taking the woman into account.

Now you understand what confidence really is and why the Jerk seems to have more of it than you do. Hopefully, you also know that your hesitation is not a sign of weakness, but it is a sign that you care. Do not forget this next time you feel bad for hesitating out of consideration.

CHAPTER SIX

NICE GUY PARANOIA

Lucky Nice Guy

Did you get lucky last night? This expression is often used by Nice Guys when they are asking someone, if they met a new woman last night, or more commonly, when asking did they have sex last night. If a Nice Guy is in a relationship with a woman he will often think to himself or believe, *Wow, she is amazing; I am so lucky she is with me.* They use the term "lucky" because they believe that fate has decided to reward them and they are grateful for meeting that new woman, having sex, or being in that relationship.

Feeling lucky to be in relationship/interaction places the Nice Guy in extreme danger of Nice Guy paranoia. Many Nice Guys who experience Nice Guy paranoia become overly preoccupied with losing a woman because they feel lucky to be with her. The problem with feeling lucky in a relationship is that we feel as if we have very little control. It is not healthy to be in a relationship where we feel like we have little control or influence over it. When you think you have no control over a relationship, then you feel like you are at the mercy of forces outside of your control.

Luck relies on chance, timing, and opportunity, and those three things are beyond most people's control. The Nice Guy who experiences "Nice Guy paranoia," does so many times because if he does not know how he got his woman. And then he does not know how to keep her. When you do not know how something works, then you do not know how to fix it when it is broken, or you do not know how to make that thing do what you want it to do.

☢

Signs you may be in danger of letting your paranoia control you:

Feel lucky she is with you

Don't know why she is with you

Think she is perfect, not just perfect for you, but perfect

Feel like she chose you and you do not know why

Do not feel as if you are good enough for her

Are threatened by every guy she interacts with significantly

Thinks she is what makes you who you are

Feel as though you have little or no influence on her staying with you or leaving you

Do not have a life and or interest outside of her

You are threatened by her spending time around her friends and or family

There is an expression that says it is better to be lucky than it is to be good. There are two problems with relying on luck: One, you cannot duplicate your success. Two, it is not sustainable. Often the price of being lucky is accepting that you have little or no control over what has/or will happen. This lack of control is what leads to the paranoia, which many Nice Guys feel.

The lucky Nice Guy issue is magnified for the Nice Guy because he also has self-esteem issues because of the Conspiracy. The problem is that feeling lucky and inferior at the same time is a very dangerous place to be mentally, especially when in a relationship. Nice Guy paranoia means you are always worried and stressing about losing your woman to forces beyond your control. We all know paranoia, fear, shame, doubt, and an inferiority complex are the perfect combination for an unhealthy and unstable relationship.

This example illustrates how Nice Guy paranoia works perfectly in a relationship:

What if you were walking along and found the Holy Grail? What would you think? At first you would probably think to yourself, *Oh my,*

I can't believe my luck, I cannot believe I found the grail. At first you would probably be ecstatic. Then after the initial euphoria wears off, you would probably start to wonder: *What did I do to deserve this? What makes me so special for me to keep the Holy Grail in my possession?*

There are tens of thousands of people on the planet who are more deserving of something like this: a historian, a priest, a museum collector, anyone but you. I bet you would eventually be consumed with thoughts of people with more grail experience, grail knowledge, financial resources, and an utter lack of respect for your relationship to the grail, all trying to take the grail from you. You may even wonder, *What right do I have to keep something as special as this all to myself?*

You would feel this paranoia because you' would feel lucky you got by with it. You believe if you lost the grail then you would have no idea how to get it back because you do not know how you got it in the first place. A part of you may even believe you do not deserve to keep it because it was too special for you to have it in the first place. This is an example of what a Nice Guy feels when he is experiencing Nice Guy paranoia.

The reason why you would feel this paranoia is because you are at the mercy of forces outside of your control. You had no control in getting the grail, and as a result, you have no control in keeping it. It is the same with women if you do not know why she is with you, or if you feel that you are lucky to be with her. You feel as if you have no control over your situation.

The Jerk and The Lucky Nice Guy

One especially painful reality for most Nice Guys is they feel romantically and sexually inferior when they compare themselves to the Jerk. We all know women have been trained to think that Nice Guys are great for hanging out at the park, going shopping with, helping with homework, changing a tire, babysitting her kids for her while she and her friends go out to party, etc. In other words, Nice Guys are great for anything and everything that is non-romantic and nonsexual. Why? Well to put it bluntly, because the general consensus is that Jerks are better in bed than Nice Guys. This is true in many aspects of our culture; we are constantly being told that the Jerk is cool and sexy. We are told the Jerk always gets the girl, and the Nice Guy always gets to watch the Jerk get the girl.

It is hard to argue with the theory that in this culture we automatically confuse the Jerk's "so-called" aggressiveness with his "so-called" sexual prowess. Jerks are constantly accepted and recognized as sexually superior to the Nice Guy. Very few Nice Guys ever confront this reality head on; they just quietly accept their "inferior" position without fully understanding why society accepts this as true.

The end result of all this constant reinforcement of the Nice Guy's alleged inferior position is what causes, "Jerk paranoia." Jerk paranoia happens when the Nice Guy becomes overly preoccupied with losing a woman to a Jerk. The main problem is that this preoccupation often will turn to fear, which will lead to paranoia. What happens is because he thinks he is inferior to the Jerk, he will become overly preoccupied with losing her to the Jerk. This happens most often when the average Nice Guy is involved with a woman who he values, especially one who he sees as having more value than him.

The intensity of this Jerk paranoia is usually based on how much he values the woman. The more he cares about the woman, or the perceived value she has, not only to him, but to other guys out there, the more paranoid he is about losing her. Her value to the Nice Guy can be based on anything, looks, personality, money, status, etc.

Every Nice Guy's secret fear is that the woman he is with, or that he is interested in, will cross paths with some perceived to be sexually superior. Namely, an immoral, uncaring, undisciplined Jerk who has no issue at all with trying to take his woman from him. The reason why he fears the Jerk is because he does not know how to stop him. That lack of knowledge, coupled with a lack of self-esteem, is the reason why many Nice Guys can come across as jealous, possessive, always on edge, controlling, insecure, etc. This is because men know whenever you have something of value, you will also have competition for it. People may eventually come around and try to take that valuable object. Nice Guys know or believe that these Jerks will stop at nothing to get their women: they will, lie, cheat, say, and do anything to get what they want. The Nice Guy feels all of this, and he feels powerless to stop it. What this can lead to is the Nice Guy becoming overprotective of his woman. This is how he, she, and the relationship and/or interaction becomes held hostage by this paranoia.

The best way to fight Nice Guy paranoia or Jerk paranoia is with knowledge. The best way to get knowledge in this case is communication with the woman who is causing you to feel lucky and/or paranoid. Ask her why she likes you. Ask her what she thinks is attractive about you. You can even tell her some variation of, "I feel lucky that I am with you, and the problem with feeling lucky is that I have no control over it. Knowledge equals control, and I have no way to make you happy without knowledge about you, so tell me about you so I can make you happy."

CHAPTER SEVEN

THE PERFECTION SYNDROME AND THE NICE GUY

If you hear the same message about yourself all day everyday then you will tend to believe it. This is what is happening to Nice Guys when it comes to how they see themselves. Nice Guys are constantly told by the Conspiracy to be dissatisfied with who they are and how they see themselves. They don't just come out and say it like this, they are a lot more subtle. You may know these phrases and slogans:

No excuses

Change your life

Be the perfect new you

Live your best life

It's time for a new you

Be somebody special

Live with no regrets

Make your life extraordinary

It is extremely difficult to read any of these and feel completely satisfied with your life. That is because those slogans imply that if your life is not perfect then there must be something wrong with you. The question you should ask yourself is how can you let someone who does not know you tell you not to like yourself or your life? Most people are not dissatisfied with their whole life, just parts of it. For someone who does not know anything about you to tell you that you need a new life is almost disrespectful to you. Would you accept a total stranger coming up to you and telling you that you need a new body or a new girlfriend or a new car without telling you how they came to that conclusion? Most people would not.

But many Nice Guys automatically accept what television ads, magazine covers, gurus, and perfect strangers tell you about yourself as true.

The most disturbing thing about their advice is that they do not even know you. This would be like a doctor giving you his diagnosis without even examining you to see what is wrong with you. You would not automatically accept a doctor's blind diagnosis, so why would you accept a perfect stranger's? The reason why most Nice Guys fall for this trick is because this is a very old manipulation tactic that has been designed to work on people like you since before you were born.

This tactic is what is known as a "cold read." As far as Militant Nice Guy is concerned, a cold read is a technique used by those who do not know you, for the purpose to gain instant authority and credibility with you by convincing you that they know something unique or specific to you. The way they do it is by taking information that is true for most people, and framing or wording it in a way where it comes across as if they are talking about you specifically. This is done so that you think they know more about you than they really do.

Examples of cold reads:

You feel guilty because you know there are days when you could be more productive with your time

You are a good person, but you do not trust people when you first meet them.

You have a hard time balancing what you should or have to do with what you want to do.

You have a kind heart, but I can tell you hate guys who are mean to women.

I can tell overall that you are satisfied with your life, but there are some things you would love to go back and change.

These statements are true for most people on the planet, but they are phrased in such a way to make it seem as if they are only talking about you. This is the essence of a cold read. The reason why cold reads work when it comes to the perfection syndrome and the Nice Guy is because it is playing on the natural dissatisfaction many Nice Guys have with some parts of their lives. That dissatisfaction is used to manipulate you.

Almost everyone is dissatisfied with some parts of their life. At some point in life this is natural and to be expected. Nice Guys have been trained to believe that they and their life should be perfect all the time, and if it is not, then there must be something wrong with them or their life. The Conspiracy plays on their natural dissatisfaction with their false promise of a carefree, worry free, stress free, life. They compare your so-called "problem filled" life with promises of perfection. The end result is to get you to the point where you believe something is wrong because you do not have a perfect life and you need to change who you are, or your life, as a result.

Penis enlargement advertisements are the perfect example of this perfection syndrome. Let's look at an example of how some of these ads can work. It would be a safe bet to assume that most men are not one hundred percent secure in the size of their penis. So if an ad's headline asked you, "Do you have a big penis", most men at best would be unsure how to answer. This is in part because there is not a set definition of what constitutes a big penis. At that moment of slight uncertainty they have you. This is what the ad wants from you, uncertainty, and it uses this uncertainty to create doubt.

Most advertisements then agitate your doubt with some variation of the following question: "Do you give your woman mind-blowing orgasms every time you have sex?" Once again, you, at best, are unsure how to an- swer because you do not know the definition of mind-blowing orgasms. And, if you give her mind-blowing orgasms, now you have to do it every time, which is not possible even with a "big penis," so you have to answer, "No." And what they have very subtly done is tie her sexual satisfaction to the size of your penis. The penis enlargement companies want and need you to be dissatisfied with the size of your penis, because if you are not dissatisfied then you will not buy any products from them.

To further see how deep this manipulation goes, it does not even matter if you do not buy their product, because by then the damage is already done. The advertisement has already affected you. The next time you have sex and do not give your woman mind-blowing or- gasms (which still has not been defined, and is impossible to do every time even if it was defined) you may be tempted to blame the size of your penis, thus confirming the need in your head for the pills. So, the next advertisement airs, you will be in a much better position to buy next time, (whether or not it is the same advertiser). Even if you do not ever buy any penis enlargement pills, the damage is still done to you psychologically.

This is the same with the Conspiracy, it makes you doubt yourself, it plays on your natural dissatisfaction and frustration that all people have with some parts of their lives, and uses it against you. Helping you is not their main concern; their main concern is to make you feel bad for not being perfect and having a perfect life. They want you to feel incomplete or that you need to change who you are. If they were really interested in helping you, then they would not arrogantly and automatically presume to know you need a new life without knowing who you are first as a person.

You are told to live your best life, or to always be the best, but they never tell you what that means exactly. As a result, you are left to judge yourself by the standard of perfection or an ideal of what you think "being the best" means. Because this goal is either poorly defined and/or vague, you will fail every time. Also, because your goal is vague (live your best life) you will never fully know when you have reached that goal, so you are much more vulnerable to being dissatisfied with yourself. How can you truly know if you are being the best you can be if you never define what that is for yourself?

To effectively help someone improve their life, you would first figure out where they currently stand, and what exactly they wanted to change, and then give them a clear plan to get there. You would have to find out what they have to do to reach their goal, or what is keeping them from their goal. It would greatly benefit Nice Guys to understand significant change is often an extensive process that takes time, effort, and often trial and error. It is easier to get people to doubt themselves simply by stating if your life is not perfect, then something must be wrong with you. There is nothing wrong with you.

The best option when confronted with the perfection syndrome is to realize that it is impossible to be perfect all the time. The moment Nice Guys realize they do not have to have a perfect life or have a perfect interaction with a woman, is the moment they start to accept what is really happening to them, They will be well on their way to appreciating their interactions. This is because they are not judging themselves against the impossible standard of perfection.

Success, the Nice Guy and Women

The Conspiracy has convinced many Nice Guys to falsely believe that to interact with women successfully, you not only have to have your life figured out, but it has to be a successful life, filled with purpose and meaning. When you have "all this figured out," then that will make you more attractive to women. This is a major reason why many Nice Guys feel they need to be a success first before they can interact with women in a significant way. However, there are a couple of major problems with this line of thinking:

For starters, success is often poorly defined. Very few people on this planet really know and can state with certainty what a successful life looks like. If this is the case, then how do you know when you are successful enough to talk to women?

And from a practical standpoint, what are you suppose to do in the mean time, while you are in the process of becoming successful? If you follow the Conspiracy's advice, then that will either mean: a) not talking to women until you become a success, or b) you will have to struggle with your interactions with women until you find success or a life's purpose, then all of your problems with women will disappear and you will magically become good with women.

Both of these assertions are simply not true. You know this because you personally know too many directionless, underachieving, purposeless Jerks who are with women you want to be with, and are having sex with the women you want to have sex with. You know you have (or had) more going for you than these many of these Jerks, and still the women choose them over you. And what about all of the successful guys you know who are not doing so well with women? What happened to the magic powers over women they were suppose to possess?

The truth of the matter is there are no magic powers; success in one area of your life has little to do practically with the other. This is not to say that success in one area of your life does not help you to achieve success in another area, but those times, when it does happen to work out, are often incidental. There are plenty of guys who do get results with women because they are a success. No one is denying that having a good job, or a lot of money, or something about yourself that you are proud of or being a success does make interacting with women easier. The problem

94

is the women you get as a result of being a success are the residual benefits of being successful and not the primary goal of that success.

It is not an effective plan for you if you feel the need to be a success, and/or your best or perfect before you do something as simple as interact with a woman. This is not productive for you, because you are telling yourself, subconsciously, that you do not think you are generally good enough to talk to women as you already are. When you constantly tell yourself you are not good enough to talk to women, then you will take yourself out of the game before you even have a chance to play, or if you do decide to play, then your lack of belief in self will affect your performance.

Your Are Not Your Job, or Are You?

In part, our definition of ourselves is often some form of a combination of our goals, principles, and what we primarily take pleasure in doing. Sometimes that may or may not include our jobs and/or our possessions. Many Nice Guys believe that their jobs and their possessions automatically define or determine who they are as a man. They believe if they can get a certain job or get the right stuff., then they will be happy.

☢

They believe that being a:

Businessman	is what makes you successful
Musician	is what makes you sexy
Actor	is what makes you cool
Dancer	is what makes you attractive to women
Politician	is what makes you important
Doctor	Is what makes you smart
Artist	is what makes you mysterious
Photographer	is what makes you interesting

This type of thinking is why many Nice Guys take on jobs and careers they really are not passionate about and perform tasks they do not like. They hang around people they cannot stand, because they are letting their job and/or status, automatically define who they are as a person. This is because they are choosing who they want to be based on someone else's standards, and not their own. They are looking for their jobs and possessions to give their lives meaning. What many Nice Guys do not realize is that we give our jobs and possessions meaning, not the other way around.

People, especially Nice Guys, mistakenly automatically think their jobs are who they are, or their possession are what define them. This may or may not be the case. If you take pleasure at your job then it may be so, but this does not necessarily have to be the case. In many cases, our jobs are the sacrifice or the financial support, which enables us to do what we really love, or want. Our jobs may give us a chance to be who we really want to be.

☢

Below are examples of Nice Guys defining what their jobs mean to their identity:

He works in a cubicle so he can teach salsa part time

He enjoys cooking so he became a chef

He is a teacher during the school year so that he can travel in the summer

He is a night watchman so can go to school during the day

He wants to keep his family safe so he became a policeman

He wants to be a good father financially so he works two jobs

Our identity does not necessarily, or automatically. have to be wrapped up in our jobs; it is up to each one of us to make this choice for ourselves.

Let's take a high school teacher who also teaches salsa. Would that person identify themselves as a high school teacher or a salsa instructor, or both? It is entirely up to that person to choose how they want to identify themselves. It is not the job that defines you, you choose how you want to define yourself; you are who you chose to be.

Those who would tell you that you are not your job, are usually not happy with the job they have. Believe it or not, but there are people out there who do love their jobs, for example: athletes, businessmen, actors, doctors, dancers, etc. Furthermore, some of these people not only love their jobs, but choose to identify themselves by their job and are happy to do so. I have a friend who is so proud of being a doctor that he prefers for people to refer to him as Dr. Stevens, and he seems at peace with himself and who he is.

A major reason why some people are happy to identify with their jobs, and others are not, usually comes down to choice. The ones who feel as if they have a choice in how they identify themselves are usually happier because they have some say in that decision and they know what it is they are choosing to be. Those athletes, businessmen, actors, doctors and dancers etc. not only chose this path, but suffered, struggled, and sacrificed, to one day have their identity. So do not listen to those who say you are not your job.

In the past, most professional football players did not make enough money playing football to support themselves, and many had to get jobs in the off season to help pay the bills. Now, if you had asked them how they identified themselves, I am sure they would have said they were football players primarily, and not car salesmen, teachers, construction workers, or whatever job they chose to help support themselves in the off season. Their summer job was to only help them to be better football players.

If you enjoy playing football, and you play football, then you are a football player. Your choice of defining yourself as a football player is not dependent on if you have a part-time job and play football on the weekends, that does not matter, what matters is how you identify yourself. That is especially true now. Although many football players make more money than they could ever spend playing football, many of these players still take up jobs in the off-season to make more money. They do everything from selling shoes, to acting, to owning restaurants. Yet when they and others identify them, they are identified primarily as football players. How do you choose to be identified?

How Nice Guys Lose Their Identity In Systems

Another major reason Nice Guys do not like themselves is because they do not trust themselves. When Nice Guys do not trust themselves or believe in themselves, then they will often seek out something outside of themselves to believe in. They will try to find some method, tools, or belief system to trust to make up for their lack of belief in self.

For the purposes of this book, trusting yourself means that you are able to read a situation and read yourself and respond appropriately to that situation. For example, you trusting yourself when it comes to meeting and or interacting with women means you believe you have the ability to favorably influence the outcome of an interaction you chose to have with her. Also, that you know how to handle the consequences when the outcome does not go exactly as planned.

When one does not know or like who they are, then they are extremely vulnerable and susceptible to these methods and techniques they are learning, taking over their identity.

What happens is that Nice Guys start to become what their methods and techniques tell them to be, or what they think the stereotype of those methods tells them to be. As a result, they are in grave danger of becoming a slave to the method, or what they think the method represents.

This is really evident when someone becomes obsessed with learning a new skill, or joins a new social or religious group. Often times they will take on the stereotype of what they think that skill or organization represents to them. Let's take learning how to fight for example; an interesting thing happens when a lot of new guys with no identities or no real goals first learn how to fight, what often happens in the beginning of their learning is that they start sizing everyone up. They will judge other people and their value based on how well they can fight, or they may start trying to act tough and intimidating, and maybe even start to bully people they know they can beat up. They do this because they think this how they are supposed to act. They do not know what to do with their tools so they let the tools define them

Now let's take a look at someone who learns some new methods or ways of dating women from a dating coach. They may think to themselves, I have these new skills, so let me go out and pick-up women. Then they go out and proceed to try out their new skills on random women. They have no real agenda other than to pick them up because they think they can, or they want to experiment with their new skills, or they want to pick her up for the academic exercise of "getting her."

These two are perfect examples of someone who is letting their skills define who they are. If the guys in these examples knew who they were and what they wanted, then they would not be going around using their skills just for the hell of it. The fighter would know why and/or who he wanted to fight and let his skills serve who he is, and his goal. He can use us skills to fight for pleasure, to protect himself, for profit, or to be a bully. The guy learning how to attract women will know the type of women he wants to attract. He can use his skill to meet interesting women, or he can use his skills to trick a woman into sex. It is up to the individual to determine how he will use his skills.

Now here is something important to understand when you are learning a new skillset or new techniques, there is often a certain time period, usually in the beginning where you have to devote yourself totally to learning its teachings or methods. What this means is that you may have to put your identity on hold temporally in order to get the technique perfected, or the system mastered. Then after this temporary stage, you should reassert who you are to make the system work for you, your goals and/or your wants.

Let's take for example a bodybuilder who wants to learn a boxing workout to help him to lose weight. While he is learning the technique of how to train like a boxer, he may have to suspend his bodybuilding workout temporarily. He will resume his bodybuilding workouts after he learns how to competently execute a boxing workout. Then the bodybuilder will be able to incorporate his newly-learned boxing techniques into his bodybuilding workout, to help him become a better bodybuilder. When you know who you are and/or what you want, then it becomes more difficult for you to be taken over by your tools and methods. Nice Guys who know who they are and what they want, will use their methods and techniques to help them to serve who they are instead of the other way around.

CHAPTER EIGHT

THE ALPHA MALE AND THE NICE GUY

This section of the book is devoted to one of the most insidious weapons the Conspiracy has at its disposal. That is the concept of the alpha male. This weapon has arguably manipulated and controlled more Nice Guys directly and indirectly than any weapon in the Conspiracy's arsenal. We will highlight some of the many ways the Nice Guy has been damaged by the alpha male concept.

You and The Term "Alpha Male"

First of all, let's look at the name, alpha male, it just sounds cool when you say it out loud. Unfortunately, many Nice Guys just accept that being alpha is the way to be, simply because it sounds cool without them ever understanding exactly what the term "alpha" means.

This is because the very term alpha male encourages immediate unquestioning acceptance of the alpha male concept. Why would you want to be a regular male when you can be an alpha male? This is kind of like buying detergent, who wants the regular strength detergent when you can buy the one with extra strength? The name, "alpha male," automatically slants your perception in one of an automatic acceptance of the alpha male concept without even thinking critically about what that means for you.

The concept of the alpha male has many different names in many different cultures, societies, and situations. Different names for the alpha male:

Leader	Dominate one
Main man	Head honcho
Big dog	Boss
The Don	The Man
The King	Mack

From here on out, this book will use the term alpha male or alpha as an umbrella term to encompass all of the other terms.

The reason this is being emphasized is because this is a very important part of how the Conspiracy manipulates you with the alpha male concept. They do this through something called, "glittering generalities." These are words and phrases designed to bypass your logic and reasoning and appeal directly to your emotions. The terms used to describe the traits of the alpha male are full of glittering generalities.

☢

Some terms used to describe the alpha male:
    Natural leader
    Strong
    Knows what he wants
    Confident
    Good with women
    Powerful
    Charismatic
    Center of attention

All of these terms used to describe an alpha male are designed to evoke a good feeling rather than convey information. The Conspiracy wants you to turn off your logic and think only with your emotions. Who can be against any of the words and phrases on this list, they make you feel good?

Nice Guys have been manipulated to believe that they are not good enough as they are. Because of this perceived fear, Nice Guys are constantly looking for the edge, any piece of information, or way to behave, to make them more efficient. The Conspiracy puts the alpha male bait out there for the Nice Guys to take. The Nice Guy takes the alpha male bait because of its promise to end his frustration, not only with women, but with him trying to figure out who he is as a man.

How the Beta Male is Hurting You

A very important weapon when someone is trying to manipulate anyone is to have an enemy or someone to fight against. Nothing bonds people together faster than an adversary or an enemy for one to fight against. This is the function of the beta male concept. The Conspiracy uses the beta male concept as a powerful weapon against the Nice Guy. The Conspiracy wants you to fear the beta male concept so you will automatically fight against it without question.

Very few Nice Guys understand what it truly means to be beta. All they really know about the beta male is to fear it and that being a beta male, or exhibiting so-called beta behavior is bad for you, and that you need to resist being one at all cost.

The beta male concept also influences you by discouraging your opposition to the alpha male concept. All opposition to the alpha male mentality, legitimate or otherwise, is automatically labeled as beta behavior or beta thinking. As a result, labeling the one who dared to question the alpha male concept as a beta male, or behaving like a beta, implying they are flawed or weak. What this does is discourage the Nice Guy from thinking for himself and from asking critical question about the alpha male concept.

☢

Some terms used to describe the beta male:
Follower
Weak
Indecisive
Lacks confidence
Bad with women
Shy
Quiet

The beta male concept does nothing for us practically other than serve as our own personal "boogie man," or police force appointed to us by the Conspiracy to scare, guilt, bully, shame, force, or keep us in line. If the Conspiracy were to remove the threat of the beta male concept, then the alpha mentality would lose much of its power. You should be leery of any belief system that must have its own emotional Gestapo in place to keep you in line.

Inferior Beta Male

If you have heard anything about the alpha male, then you no doubt have heard about the mountains of so-called "scientific" and "biological evidence," which supports the alpha male concept. You have no doubt heard some variation of the scientific/biological belief that women are biologically hardwired to want the alpha male and to have sex with the alpha male because he has stronger genes. It has been said that women, because they have been trained or hardwired since the caveman days, have no choice but to be attracted to and mate with the stronger more powerful and more dominant alpha male. The beta male just has to accept his inferior position in society, with the alpha male, and with women. The beta male must do this because it is the alpha male's natural right, he is superior. Who are we to go against science and biology?

If this is true, then what does that say about you if you are this supposed beta male? Think about the logic of this line of thinking for a second, if there is scientific/biological evidence that women are attracted to alpha males, and if women are not attracted to you as a Nice Guy, then this makes you by definition a beta male. So, if you believe in the alpha male mentality, then you have no choice, but to accept your permanent inferior position.

Here is something many Nice Guys do not realize, you do have a choice. You can either a) choose to accept the alpha male concept that you are biologically and scientifically inferior, or b) you can choose to reject the idea that you are inferior, and that you do not deserve your second-class status that has been put upon you by the Conspiracy via the alpha male concept.

You may ask, but what about the mountains of "so-called" scientific and biological information, which states beta males are inferior and are destined not to be good with women? Well, instead of wasting our precious time getting distracted trying to refute each of these "so-called" scientific findings, I ask you to simply look at history. If you study the history of most oppressors, you will see they all have used this very same method to keep themselves in power.

Virtually, all oppressors see themselves as better than the people they are trying to oppress and/or manipulate. They often believe some variation of the following: that they are genetically superior, or more divine, royal, advanced, or they have a natural right to lead. How many different races, genders, people with different sexual orientations, religious, and ethnic backgrounds, have you seen this happen throughout history?

So why would you think this is not happening to you right now. This is consistent with how the Conspiracy operates. They want to convince you there is something wrong with you so that you will take yourself out of the game. The Conspiracy does not have to worry about stopping you if you already think that you are inferior to them, or something is wrong with you.

When you tell yourself that you want to be an alpha male and accept the alpha male concept, then you are doing a great disservice to yourself by putting yourself at a tremendous disadvantage. This is because once you accept the alpha male mentality, then you must know that what you are doing on some level is telling yourself that you believe that you are not good enough as you are, or that you think you have to be someone or something else .

Alpha Male or Die

Another side effect of the vague definition of both the alpha male and beta male that it often causes the Nice Guy to start to develop an idealized alpha self and idealized beta self. Because of this, he will judge himself based on those standards, that is he will judge himself based on vague ideals of what he thinks those terms mean. He will start to judge whether or not his behavior is alpha or not, or he may start to think, Hey, this is beta behavior, and I do not want to do that.

Nice Guys may start to compare their idealized selves to their normal selves. What this does is causes the Nice Guy to judge their behavior based on who or what they think they should be as vaguely defined by someone else, and not by their own standards. There are many Nice Guys who have fallen for this alpha male or die mentality. Many have been unnecessarily led to believe that they are not enough as they are simply because they are not alpha.

The major issue with adopting the alpha male mindset is it encourages an "either/or" mindset. This is where you are forced to have to choose between either being a strong alpha male or a weak beta male. The Conspiracy uses the alpha male mentality to take the focus off of improving you and places it on trying to convince you to join their way of thinking, or become what they want you to become, which is not necessarily a better you. The Conspiracy tells you that you can be anything you want to be, as long as it an alpha male. If you choose to accept the alpha male mentality for yourself, then at least define what that term means for you. Do not let others define it for you. This is a way you can use the concept of the alpha male to help you to be a better Nice Guy.

CHAPTER NINE

EXPRESSION

This section is dedicated to examining some of the common issues that Nice Guys have to deal with when they are trying to express
themselves. This section on expression is important because most Nice
Guys do not realize there is nothing fundamentally wrong with what
they want to express. The major reason why Nice Guys have such a hard
time expressing themselves is simply because Nice Guys on the whole
are inefficient at expressing themselves, primarily because of the of a
lack of belief in self.

When people do not have any faith or do not believe in how they
feel, then they will tend to express themselves ineffectively and/or
inefficiently. Because the Nice Guy is often ineffective at expressing
himself, he will often confuse this ineffectiveness within him. He may
think there is something wrong with who he is as a person or with
what he has to say, and as a result, he will be in danger of not liking
himself. The ironic thing is that a major part of communicating effectively is liking who you are. Because if you do not believe that you are
someone worth communicating with, then chances are you will be a
poor communicator.

The reason why effective expression is important is because humans
are social creatures, and an important part of who we are as people
is how we relate to and interact to each other. To deny ourselves the
ability to express ourselves effectively to others can be torturous to us.
That is why in prison one of the most effective weapons used to punish
hardened inmates is solitary confinement. Most people have a hard time
dealing with loss of human contact if it is not by choice.

In order to properly express yourself, you have to know what you
want, how you are feeling, and knowledge of who you are as a person.

Why You Feel Like You Are Bothering Women

I was having a question and answer session after a seminar I was giving. One of the attendees told me he was having a problem approaching women in the gym. He said women like to wear ear buds when they workout. He wondered what he could do to get a woman to take out her ear buds so he could talk to her. I told him to simply ask her to take out her ear buds so she could listen to him talk to her. He told me that no woman wants some boring guy to walk up to her and bother her with his conversation. I told him if that is how he sees himself when he approaches a woman, then he is correct, he is probably going to be bothering her.

Simply put, if you feel like you are bothering a woman when you are considering approaching her, then you probably are a bother. Chances are if you were not about to bother her, then you would not feel as if you were. What if you had some good news to tell her, would you feel like you were bothering her then? If your intention is sincere, that is if you want to improve her day in some way, would you let those ear buds stop you?

What if I gave you a check for five hundred dollars, and told you to give it to the best-looking woman in the gym, and you thought it was her? How would you feel about approaching her now, how would you feel about yourself? Would you feel like you were bothering her then? Would you be hesitant to ask her to take out her ear buds, I bet you would not.

That is because you know for a fact that you are adding value to her day. What woman would not want five hundred dollars, especially as a result of her being the best-looking woman in the gym? Even if she turned down the money, it would more than likely be more of a reflection of her, then it would be commentary on the value of the money.

Now most Nice Guys believe that they are worth much more than five hundred dollars so why would they hesitate to talk to her on their own without the check? Why would they feel like they were bothering her?

According to conventional wisdom, to bother someone means to give annoyance, to disturb, or pester. However, as far as this book is concerned, in this section, to bother someone means to try to get someone to take part in an action or activity that is less valuable or important to them than what they are doing at that moment. This is why you would not feel like you are bothering the woman at the gym with the five hundred dollar check, because you know for certain that you are adding value to her day. You would have no problem stopping her and asking her to take her ear buds out, no problem stopping her if she was walking to work, talking to her friends or whatever. That is because you know that what you have to offer is more relevant or interesting to her than what she is currently doing.

I used to be a disc jockey at a radio station, and my mentor gave me some excellent advice to determine if I was being self-indulgent and bothering the listeners or if what I was going to say or do was good enough to be put on the air. He said if the bit I was planning to air was better than the song I was going to play next, then it was safe to put it on the air. If the bit was not, then I was just bothering the listeners, and I would be better off if I just played the song.

This advice can be modified and used as simple guide to help you to determine if your feeling that you are bothering a woman is valid or not. Ask yourself if what you want to say to her or do with her is more interesting and relevant to her than what she is doing at the moment? If you think you can offer her something better than what she is doing when you want to approach her, then chances are you will not be bothering her. Now, if you think you cannot offer her something better, then you stand a strong chance of bothering her. To be able to do this requires you to know what you are bringing to the table, and to know why you want to talk to her.

This is where you have to get involved and start to calibrate yourself to each specific situation so you can learn to start trusting yourself. To do this requires you to learn how to read different situations so that you can learn if you are bothering her or not. This is not a perfect solution, nor is it meant to be, this is simply a tool to use, nothing more, or less.

For example, Let's say you overhear a woman talking to her friend about how they both want to learn salsa dancing. They are attractive, so you decide to walked up to them and introduced yourself. If you start talking to them about the weather, then you stand a very good chance of bothering them. This is because you are not adding anything to the conversation, instead, you are taking from the women. You are talking to them to please yourself at the expense of their conversation.

Now, if you were to overhear them talking about learning salsa, and you were a salsa instructor and you started talking to them about salsa, then you are not bothering them, because you are able to add value to the conservation, or because you have the ability to make their conservation. It is not necessarily because you are a salsa instructor, being a salsa instructor is only the vehicle that you could use to add value to the conversation.

Not only do you have to know what you want, you also have to be conscious of your environment. Ask yourself, *Would a woman be more receptive to hear a funny joke or an interesting story, while she is waiting for a bus or in the grocery line?* Would the anecdote be as interesting while walking to an important meeting or while she is in the middle of typing a report that is due in thirty minutes? If you want to stop her while she is walking to an important meeting or typing, then your joke or story better be really funny, interesting, important, or relevant.

Sometimes when you are unsuccessful at approaching a woman, your problems may not necessarily be that you are saying the wrong things; it may be just the wrong time for you. That is why you should learn to listen to yourself when you feel like you are bothering someone, you should try learn why you are having this feeling, not fear it. How will you ever know if your feelings are valid if you do not ever examine or explore them?

The Conspiracy will tell you to ignore your feelings, or they will say if you feel like you are bothering her, then you are just being negative. They tell you to believe that you are enough just as you are and go after what you want regardless of the consequences. Well logically, that does not makes any sense because if you follow their advice then you will never come upon a situation where you are in danger of bothering a woman who you are approaching. Now if you just think about it for a second, then you know that is not possible. Part of being an effective communicator as a Nice Guy is to know when you are bothering someone. If you do as the Conspiracy says, and ignore your thoughts, then how will you ever discover and learn if indeed you are being bothersome.

The key is not to ignore the feeling that you are bothering her, but to find out why you are having that feeling. Now this should not be used as an excuse not to approach or interact with women. Feeling as if you are bothering someone is not meant to keep you from interacting with women. It is meant for you to learn why you feel that way so you can calibrate and adjust accordingly so you will become better at interacting.

Why Nice Guys Want To Be Like Jerks

A common tactic for many Nice Guys who do not like themselves is for them to look outside themselves for answers to their problems. Now for the most part, this is very logical and rational; it makes sense. If there is something about yourself that you want to change and/or don't like, then go ahead and change it. And by all means, if you find someone you want to be like or pattern yourself after to help you get what you want in life, then go for it.

There is nothing wrong with wanting to change something about yourself as long your desire to do so occurs naturally. As long as your desire to change is of your own free will, free from trickery and influence. The problem is many Nice Guys who want change are not desiring this from their own free will. They are being tricked by the Conspiracy to hate themselves and all of their Nice Guy ways. If you take this approach, all you are doing is wanting to be like Jerk. You are foolishly envious of him. This is in large part because he has always beaten you, and other Nice Guys like you when it comes to being successful with women.

It makes perfect sense that you are jealous of him. You want what he has: his self-confidence, his arrogance with women, his seeming ability to not care and still get the girl. Many Nice Guys in many ways admire the Jerk's ability with women. No one can blame you for wanting to be a success with women. So you do what you think you need to do to finally get what you want—become a Jerk.

You know what they say, if you can't beat them, join them. So what do you, and a lot of Nice Guys like you do? You try to join them. You want to become one of these Jerks, or you may think you need a new image; or think you want to be more cool, or more of a bad-ass because you don't believe in yourself. Many Nice Guys have gone through (or will go through) the phase where they want to be like someone else. This is because they have been trained not to like themselves.

We all have either seen someone else do this, or actually have been one of these guys, trying to be someone who they (or we)are not. Sometimes it is funny, but sometimes, it can actually be sad and depressing. You may have seen these guys, they try to dress or look differently than themselves, and/or they try to talk differently than themselves. They may even try to act differently than their authentic selves. The problem is that too many Nice Guys spend way too much time trying to be someone they cannot be, and not enough time trying to make themselves more effective communicators by enhancing who they already are.

I remember when I went through one of my phases of me trying to be something I was not. I remember my all black phase. When I was younger I remember there was this guy I knew "Alec." Alec was a real Jerk, and he was good with all the ladies, and I wanted to be like him because of it. He was the smug superior type who was the master of the off handed putdown, he did not say much, but when he did you always felt insulted. For example one of his female friends once said to him, "Wow I feel great, I just ran eight miles today." He said, "Well, you have to start somewhere." Then there was the time a mutual friend asked him why he thought her boyfriend broke up with her. He said, Because you gained weight." I thought he was a Jerk, but all the women seemed to just eat his stuff up.

Another thing about him was that it always seemed as if he wore nothing but black clothes, leather pants, and silver jewelry. I just knew his secret to getting all of the girls was because he was wearing black and leather and silver. I knew this was going to be my key to glory with women.

So what did I do? I went out and totally converted my closet to nothing but black, leather, and all the silver jewelry I could find. I just knew as soon as the women saw me in my all black outfit with my leather pants and silver jewelry, I was going to be a big hit. I knew they would not be able to resist me. So, how did that work out for me? Well let's just say that I placed way too much faith in the power of a black leather clothing and silver jewelry when it comes to getting women. Needless to say, I did not get the type of attention I wanted from the ladies. The reason why I was not a success had nothing to do with what I was wearing; I was not successful because I was not being true to who I was. I could duplicate what he was doing, but I could never be him.

I say that I could never be him because while I could get his look, speech, and physical mannerisms down, all that turned out to be was an impression. I could never get his thought processes down, his vibe that he is put out there, his sub-communications, or what he said in between the words. Our thoughts, emotions and feelings are what drive the physical actions we see on the outside. Our actions and what is being said in between the words we speak are what the people are responding to, much more than our purely physical actions of our words alone. This is just a small example from my personal experience, to show you some of the many problems with trying to be someone who is not you.

Picking a Lifestyle or Image To Match Who You Are

Another mistake some Nice Guys make trying to transform themselves into a new image is they often pick one that is totally inappropriate for who they are and what they want. Not everyone looks good in everything, and not every look was meant for everyone. We have all witnessed far too many examples where someone's fashion choices are not congruent to who they are in life. Someone who's look is inappropriate for where they are socially. For example, we all have had runs in with the woman who want to be treated like a queen, but was dressed and acted like a slut. There is nothing wrong with dressing and acting like a slut, you should just expect to be treated like one every now and then if that is how you choose to dress. If you look like a priest and act like a priest, then guess what? You will be treated like a priest.

You also have to make sure the image you select is congruent to who you are as a person, and is congruent to your lifestyle, and what you want. If you are into sexy hot model-type women, then you will have a harder time getting a woman like that if you are dressed like an accountant and all you do is surf the internet all day long. If you want sexy hot model-type women, then you need a lifestyle that is consistent with what you want. This is not about sacrificing who you are as a person, this is more about you taking steps to put you in the best position to help you to get the type of woman you want.

Who you are and what you want and where you are has to fit together or you will have difficulties. You should not try to look like someone else, but try to look the best you can look. Try to find clothes, features, and a lifestyle that highlights and represents your best features. That is why it is important to know who you are and what want so your appearance, actions, and lifestyle are consistent with those desires. I remember a Nice Guy asked me at a conference, "How should I dress and carry myself to attract women?" I told him to dress and act like the guys who attract the type of women he is interested in attracting. This is one of many reasons why it's important to know who you are and what you want.

Are You A Con Artist or A Bluff Artist?

Value and the Nice Guy

In this section we will focus on the value we place on others relative to ourselves. Examining value is important because it plays a major role in not only how the Nice Guy chooses who he interacts with, but in how he feels about himself and those who he chooses to interact with. To help express ourselves more effectively, I encourage the Nice Guy to look at the people he values and how that perception affects how he sees and treats others, as well as himself.

We have divided this section into two main parts. The first section will cover conning and bluffing. These are the two main ways Nice Guys try to deceive someone to get what they want from them, and the role value plays in those choices. In the next section, we will look at catering and pandering. These are the two main ways Nice Guys behave with people in general, and the role that value plays in those choices as well.

While a genuine emotional connection is important in getting what you want from people, it is not necessary. There are many people who are fully capable of getting what they want from people without forming an emotional connection with that person. These people have mastered the tools and mechanics of interacting with people, that is they know how to say and/or do all the right things to get what they want from people.

What happens to many people who want to be better communicators is they learn, understand, and master the tools of communication, but they do not learn to understand, master, and like who they are. What often happens when you master the tools of communication without liking or knowing who you are is that you become really good at getting what you want while hiding who you are. Instead of using the tools to make a genuine emotional connection, which is what people do when they are proud of who they are, you will use your tools to make more efficient barriers to hide behind rather than to connect with people.

When it comes to interacting with a woman you are interested in, the issue at hand is not whether an genuine connection is necessary for a successful interaction or not. The issue is: Why is that person trying to have an interaction with a woman without having a genuine connection with her? Most people agree that having an interaction with a genuine emotional connection normally enhances their interactions. So why would someone choose to have an interaction without making a genuine emotional investment or connection?

When you use your tools to deceive someone to get what you want without forming a genuine connection, or respecting the connection that you have with that person, then you are in danger of becoming either a con or a bluff artist. There are many reasons why someone would choose to be a con artist or a bluff artist. Militant Nice Guy focuses on value.

Conning and bluffing, for the purpose of the book, simply defines two potential methods and or techniques guys use to deceive women to get what they want from them. This is done with women who guys perceive have different values from them. The main determining factor that will determine whether his deception will be a con or bluff is dependent largely on how he sees the woman's value in relation to himself. If the guy believes he has less value than her, then he will most likely try to bluff her. If he thinks he has more value than she does, then he will try to con her.

When it comes to interacting with women, a con artist is someone who deceives a woman and takes what he wants from her because he feels like he is superior to her. He believes this is his right because of his self-perceived superior position. His justification can be based on anything, on his superior social standing, position, skill, knowledge, moral superiority, etc. A con artist believes that the woman deserves to be conned because she is not equal to him. (Very few Nice Guys are con artist, but it is still important to examine how conning works).

When it comes to interacting with a woman, a bluff artist is someone who deceives a woman and takes what he wants from her because he feels inferior to her for some reason. He bluffs because he does not believe he is good enough to interact with her as he is, or that she is superior in some way to him. He bluffs to cover up his perceived inferior position. He feels justified to bluff her because he feels that if he did not, then he would never get what he wants from her on his own because he is not worth it, or does not deserve it.

An excellent way to help you to get a better understanding of the difference between a con artist and a bluff artists is to examine how they see/feel about types of women they con and/or bluff:

Guys usually feel the need to con women when they feel they are

114

superior to the woman with whom they want to interaction. Examples of the types of women who guys feel justified in conning can may include: strippers, sluts, prostitutes, women who they feel are less intelligent then they are, submissive women, or women who they think are weak. They use the woman's perceived inferior status as justification for their own actions. There is a certain level of devaluing of her going on when guys run a con. Guys have little respect for her beyond what she can do for him. If she were to find out that he was running a con on her, he would more than likely not care too much about it because he would feel as if she is beneath him.

Guys will be tempted to bluff when they feel inferior to the woman with whom they want interaction. Examples of these types of women may include: celebrities, models, strong women, smart women, "bad-girls," women in a higher status or position, and attractive women. Guys feel justified in bluffing these types of women because they feel as if this is the only way to get what they want from them. They do not believe in themselves enough to tell her the truth. There is a certain level of worship, or intimidation that a guy feels when he is running a bluff. He would likely feel embarrassed if she found out that he was trying to bluff or trick her. This would cause him to feel as if she found out his secret, which he is not good enough for her.

The reason why there are so many systems that teach guys to either con or bluff women to get what they want from them, is because conning and bluffing, or deceiving someone, can actually work. However, there are several side effects when it comes to prolonged use of the conning and/or bluffing mindset. *Militant Nice Guy* focuses on the difficulty you may have making a genuine emotional connection when you are conning and/or bluffing someone.

Making a genuine emotional connection with someone is difficult when you are trying to con them. This is because it is difficult to connect to someone who you feel superior to. When you see someone as beneath you, then it will be very difficult for you to identify with them and connect with them on the same level. Conning someone places you in an aggressive, manipulative mindset, and that is not a healthy mindset to be in when you want to genuinely connect with someone.

You may get what you want from the person you are conning, but it will be extremely difficult to have a genuine emotional connection with that person. Think about certain strippers who con guys out of money.

They flatter, insinuate, manipulate, and seduce money from a guy, but do you think they have connected emotionally in any meaningful way with those guys once they have taken their money? Of course not, these strippers go home and connect with people they have genuine personal bonds with.

Bluffing makes connecting with someone difficult, because it is difficult to connect to someone to whom you feel inferior. When you see someone as above you, it is extremely difficult to connect with them because you do not feel worthy to be equal to them. When you are bluffing someone you are constantly in a defensive, suspicious, protective mindset, which is unhealthy for a genuine emotional connection.

When you bluff you always live in fear of being found out, and you constantly view her every remark and/or action as a potential threat, because you are living in fear. This is why guys who try to pretend they are someone who they are not, (or those who are faking it until they make it) have an extremely hard time forming genuine connection with women.

For example, let's pretend you were bluffing about being rich. Now if a woman were to ask you what kind of car you drove, or what do you do for a living, you would see those questions as threatening. You would be on guard about those questions because these questions would have the potential to uncover your bluff. Now, if you were really rich and she asked you those questions, then you would not view them as a threat because those are natural questions, which rich guys get asked all of the time. So if you are trying to bluff about how cool you are or that you are some party guy, then it won't work in the long run because if you are really not the person who you are bluffing to be, then you will not be congruent, and you will eventually be discovered, or live in fear of being discovered.

Conning and bluffing someone is also damaging to the woman in question. Many times a woman will feel victimized and/or used when she finds out that she has been conned. She may also feel you took advantage of her. If she finds out she has been the victim of a bluff then she will feel disappointed, because her whole interaction with the guy has been based on a lie. In both cases, the woman was trying to make a genuine emotional connection with you, and that connection for her was based in part on her thinking that you were doing the same thing, but you were not.

The Catering Mindset and Its Effect on The Nice Guy

Another possible side effect of living with the low self-esteem, which the Conspiracy has put on you, is that it can encourage you to develop a catering mindset. My definition of a catering mindset is when you start thinking in terms of what is the right and what is wrong way to proceed / respond and/or behave when interacting with people overall. This is not about wanting to respond and/or behave the right way because it is the right thing to do, or because it is who you are as a person, it is based on trying to behave a certain way to get someone else's approval.

The catering mindset usually manifests itself when the Nice Guy is trying to please people who they perceive as having more value than them. Examples of these types of people may include: politicians, movie stars, the rich, beautiful women etc. Having a catering mindset is based on you trying to please the other person (woman) at the expense of the truth, or what you believe. You are primarily concerned with responding to please the other person, and/or to avoid giving the wrong answer or response as opposed to telling the truth or staying true to your values.

☢

Examples of questions that are likely to cause the catering mindset:

The bully asking, "Did you eat my cookie?"
A policeman asking, "Were you speeding?"
Your boss asking, "Were you late for work today?"
A female celebrity asking, "Are you hitting on me?"

The answer to these questions are clear, any hesitation when it comes to answering these questions are most likely the result of you not wanting to answer because you don't want to displease the person asking the question. This is an ineffective mindset to have, not only when it comes to women, but in how you express yourself overall. If you only limit yourself to thinking in pleasing or non pleasing terms, then you are not open to the natural outcome that may come from expressing yourself naturally. The following is a perfect example of a catering mindset: One of the most popular question men want the answer to is, "What should I tell a woman when she asks me how old I am?" Any man who asks this question is more than likely not secure in his age and is looking for the "right" answer to give to please the woman asking the question. He already knows the answer to her question, his real dilemma is not what the correct answer is; his real dilemma is how he can answer the question so that his answer will please her.

Common responses some Nice Guys give who have a catering mentality when asked how old they are:

Old enough to know better

Guess

Lying about their age

Old enough to know what to do and young enough to still be able to do it

Old enough

How old do I look

Asking how old is the woman instead

These may be clever responses, but if he is insecure about his age, then all those clever responses are doing is helping him to hide his insecurity while he tries to answer in a way that will please her. The reason he is hesitant to state his age is because he thinks if he gives her the "wrong" age, then she will be displeased. If he was not experiencing a catering mentality, then he would not hesitate to answer the question.

The reason why he would not hesitate to answer is because he does not have a catering mindset. If he were truly proud of his age, or if his age was of no concern to him, then he would simply answer the question as if she were asking him what his favorite color is, or what city he is from. When it comes to these questions, most Nice Guys do not have a problem with answering these questions quickly and honestly. This is because he does not think his favorite color and what city he is from will have any bearing on him getting or interacting with the woman. This is why he answers the question truthfully and quickly, because he is simply stating information or expressing himself.

When it comes to expressing yourself, having a catering mindset is a serious obstacle to you communicating authentically. When you communicate with a catering mindset, then you are prone to make decisions based on avoiding the "wrong" answer, rather than based on telling the truth, or how you feel. If you have a catering mindset, then you will consistently try to mold your answers to get her approval or avoid her displeasure. If you put yourself in this position, then you will be in a nonproductive place. More to the point, you are not expressing who you really are and what you really believe.

Instead of seeing the question of your age as some kind of pass or fail situation, you could try seeing it as a chance to give yourself some context. Being proud of who you are, (in this case your age) does not guarantee that she will not reject you based on your age, or that she may see you as a non-option romantically/sexually if she has a preference for a particular age. You being proud of your age is not suppose to stop her from seeing you in a lesser light; the point is to keep you from seeing yourself in a lesser light.

Social Protocols

Having a catering mindset is not to be confused with the fear of violating social protocols. These are two totally different issues. Social protocols are the rules and guidelines people have for how people should interact with each other. Social protocols help to determine what is acceptable and unacceptable behavior.

There are two major problems with social protocols:
1. They are often poorly defined. Social protocols are rarely agreed upon and vary from person to person, or from group to group. They also can vary from environment to environment and from culture to culture. Each of us has different social protocols that we follow and choose not to follow.

2. There is no agreed upon punishment for violation of social protocols. Also, punishments for violation often have a range of consequence, which can range from no consequences to the most severe punishment you can imagine. Punishments can even vary from person to person

for the same offense. Ignorance of social protocols often does not have any bearing on punishment.

There is nothing wrong with being fearful of expressing yourself because you fear violating social protocols. There may be real consequences as a result. Nice Guys have been trained to confuse their very legitimate fear of violation of social protocols with thinking there something wrong with them, or with weakness.

Most of the Nice Guys who hesitate to take action because they fear violating social protocols have genuine intentions. The problem is Nice Guys have been trained to see any doubt and hesitation as bad. Nice Guys would be in a much better position mentally as soon as they realize their hesitation or fear of violation of social protocols is not an issue of character, but a tactical issue.

If you are afraid of telling a coworker she looks good because you do not think she will accept a compliment from a man like you (because you think she is out of your league), is one issue. Not wanting to tell a co-worker you think she looks good because you are not sure how she would respond because of perceived sexual harassment issues, is a completely valid concern. There are possible real world consequences if she takes your compliment the wrong way.

Sincere violation of social protocols is a practical matter that is more a commentary on how you chose to proceed as oppose to commentary on who you are as a person and/or how you should see yourself. Sure, there can be practical consequences, but, Nice Guys often confuse the pain and embarrassment of violating social protocols with thinking there is something wrong with them. Just because you did something wrong, or made a mistake expressing yourself, and you violated a social protocol, does not necessarily mean that you are a bad person.

The Pandering Mindset and Its Effect on The Nice Guy

Many Nice Guys are inefficient in interacting with women they are with because they have a pandering mindset. That is, he thinks the woman has much more value than he does. And, because of this, he does not think he is worthy of being with her romantically and/or sexually. Or, he may feel he is lucky to be with her. As a result, during overall interactions, the Nice Guy will often do things that he does not want to do, or accept things he would not normally accept, just to keep her happy. The Nice Guy does this because he places more value on pleasing her than he does on himself.

Examples of Nice Guys pandering to women:
Going places they do not want to go
Spending money they do not want to spend
Talking on the phone with her for hours about some Jerk
Helping her to get a boyfriend and you want her for yourself
Taking up a hobby you are not interested in to please her

Catering Mindset vs. The Pandering Mindset

The best way to demonstrate the difference between catering and pandering is to compare how each would choose to interact with someone whom they perceive to have higher value. Let's use your favorite female celebrity for example.

Say you saw her, and the focus of your thoughts was tantamount to how amazing she is, then you would be susceptible to experiencing a catering mentality. But if you saw her and your thoughts of her caused you to either feel: turned on, impressed, inspired, excited, etc., then, you may try to do or say the right thing. Your intent would be to make her happy, or try to please her.

Now, if you were to see that celebrity and the focus or your thoughts were on yourself something along the lines of, *I am not good enough,* then you would be susceptible to using a pandering mentality. That is if you saw her and you felt, unworthy, depressed, outclassed, or over-matched. All or your actions you take with this person will be based on this pandering mentality.

Catering is a mindset based on getting a favorable response from someone you value. It is more a reflection of how you see the other person as opposed to how you see yourself. If the Nice Guy is successful with the catering mindset, then the most likely practical result may end up with him doing something he does not want to do (i.e. see a movie he does not like, hiking, take salsa lessons), and/or she believes something about him that is not true (i.e. he likes dogs, he is a democrat, he likes jazz). The long term effect on the Nice Guy if he is successful with catering to her is that he continues to believe she is more important than him.

Pandering is based on how you see you yourself relative to the other person. It is more about the unworthiness you feel about yourself as opposed to the other person. It is based on the belief that you do not deserve to be given a favorable response from someone you see as having more value than you. If the Nice Guy is successful at pandering then this will reinforce his belief that he is unworthy to have his needs met.

Pampering vs. Pandering

Now there are many Nice Guys who are legitimately happy with the woman they are with and the status of their relationship, and their desire do anything for her comes from a healthy place. Part of their enjoyment of their relationship comes from them pampering or taking care of their women.

Basically, pampering is doing something for a woman because you enjoy doing it for the sole purpose of making her happy. What is the difference between pampering and pandering? Every day far too many people have confused pandering Nice Guys with pampering Nice Guys. This confusion has resulted in many Nice Guys questioning themselves unnecessarily. Some Nice Guys have mistaken their pampering behavior with pandering behavior, and vise versa.

The reason why this happens is because pampers and panders often look alike and have the same characteristics on the outside. The only way to truly know if someone is showing pampering or pandering behavior is for guy in question to tell you. It relies on him to make his own diagnosis, and we all know the problems that come with self-diagnosis. It is nearly impossible to come up with definitive and definite rules to explain how someone feels. This is because feelings are not meant to be defined by rules and words alone. Feelings are meant to be felt, not defined. Nevertheless, here are some guidelines that you may be displaying pandering behavior.

Guidelines to show if you are pandering to a woman:

If you believe you can't say no to her request because she will like you less, or that you will lose standing with her.

Doing something you do not want to do to make her happy.

You fear that you are not worthy of asking for or receiving what you want from her and you use your behavior and/or actions to ask it for you (i.e., asking dinner to get sex instead of asking directly)

You constantly go against your better judgment to please her.

You feel uncomfortable doing things for her.

Now there is a difference between pampering and compromising. Pampering is trying to please her because it is best for her and you enjoy doing it. Compromising is pleasing her because it is best for the both of you, or for the interaction as a whole. For example, doing something you both would enjoy, such as going to a movie you both may like as opposed to going to seeing a movie which one person would hate and the other would really enjoy. The difference between pampering and compromising is small, but important.

Body language and how the Nice Guy misuses it

A common mistake many Nice Guys make with expressing themselves is that they try to use body language to make themselves more effective communicators. There is nothing wrong with wanting to use body language to help express who you are. The problem is most Nice Guys have placed far too much faith in the power and promise of body language. Many Nice Guys believe body language is the magic bullet for them getting what they want. They feel if they can use body language, or if they can learn to read body language correctly, then they will know what the woman is secretly thinking, or they try to use body language techniques to get what they want from her.

Nice Guys in particular do not have a realistic understanding of what body language can and cannot do for them. Because of this, Nice Guys often make many mistakes when they are trying to use/implement body language in their interactions. There are two mistakes

Militant Nice Guy focuses on: displaying dominance/confidence, and non congruence.

☢

Displaying Dominance/Confidence

Many Nice Guys try to use body language techniques for themselves, to try to show dominance or confidence to a woman. They think that dominant men have body language, and if they display the same type of body language, then they will be dominant, too. They may try to appear more relaxed, stand straighter, or move slower, lean back when they sit, etc.

One of my friends watched a video on how to have dominant body language, and after two weeks of intense study, he was ready to show the world his new skills. We nicknamed him, "Charlie Superhero." This is because whenever we would go out to have a good time, he would go into what we called superhero mode. He would stand at the bar with his chest out, with his hands on his hips, looking toward the heavens. Plus when he would sit down he would lean back so far until he looked like he was lying down. He did this to show how much of an alpha male he was. Apparently your "alphaness" goes up the more you lean back in your seat. Needless to say, he did not get the results he was looking for.

What "Charlie" did not understand was body language is like any language you learn such as Spanish, or German. It is supposed help you express who you are and how you feel, not be what you feel. Speaking Spanish does not make someone a Mexican, a Mexican is someone who uses Spanish to express who he is and how he is feeling. Body language is how you communicate who you are, it does not make you who you are. A confident man uses body language confidently, confident body language does not make a man confident.

☢

Non congruence

What many Nice Guys do not understand is body language works in conjunction with other factors, so his body language has to be congruent or match up with his surroundings, or what is happening around him and how he is feeling. He has to be aware of the context in which he is using or reading body language.

It would not be congruent if you told your girlfriend that you thought she was sexy in the middle of a fight, because it would be in the wrong context. Likewise, it would not be wise to smile and say hi to random people in a prison or in a tough neighborhood. There is nothing wrong with these actions in and of themselves, it is just that these are poor choices to make because these actions are not congruent with their surroundings. They do not match what is happening around them. This is where many Nice Guys make their mistakes with body language. Non congruent body language can have the same effect on how you come across, as wearing tennis shoe with a tuxedo. Although there is nothing wrong with tennis shoes in and of themselves, they just would stand out more because they are not congruent with the tuxedo.

Body language is far from an exact science, and body language is open to interpretation, environmental factors, and a certain level of empathy. Not to mention reading body language is also situational. The same movement or actions can mean different things in different situations.

For example, Nice Guys will see a woman exhibiting certain body language signals and be tempted to think: "Oh my goodness, she is touching her hair, what does that mean?", Or, they may say to themselves, "Oh no she is crossing her arms, does that means she does not like me?" Or, "Yes, she is looking down, that means that I am in a dominate position." Hypersensitivity and over reliance on reading body language often blinds the Nice Guy to other interpretations. Often, it doesn't occur to hypersensitive Nice Guys that her body language signals could mean her head itches, she is cold, and she has something in her eye. It is very difficult to get an accurate read on body language if you are obsessive about it.

☢

Are you using body language or is it using you?

You have no doubt heard some variation on the statistic that ninety percent of all communication is nonverbal. It really doesn't matter if you think that number is high or not, what is important is what drives that ninety percent with whom you communicate. That is where who you are as a person comes in to play. When it comes to expression, body language is only the physical representation of what you believe in, it is up to you to define what that means for you. Your body language is a reflection of your intent, mood, desires, your expectation of the outcome of the interaction and so much more.

Body language techniques can show you how to express your emotions more efficiently, but it cannot give you the emotions that you are expressing. Your emotions will come across naturally, unconsciously, and it is almost unnoticeable. It is the difference between hugging someone you are in love with, versus hugging your coworker. You go through the same physical motion, but the emotions are different, you can't explain the difference, but you can feel it. This is why it is extremely difficult to use body language to hide how you feel because your body language will not be congruent to how you feel, or your emotions. Now try to imagine hugging a woman you hate, but you are trying to make that woman think you love her as much as you do your girlfriend or wife. Unless you are really good at lying, then you probably can't do it. And if you did get away with it, then more than likely, you will not be able to do it for very long.

The reason why reading body language is very popular with a lot of Nice Guys is because many Nice Guys are not proud of how they feel. They feel uncertain, or just have an overall lack of confidence and faith in what they are feeling. Nice Guys believe they can hide behind body language or use it to sneak past her defenses, and worm their way into her heart. Understanding and using body language is fine in moderation, but too many Nice Guys have unrealistic expectations of what body language can and cannot do for them.

A body language expert or a book on body language is supposed to make sure you are communicating who you are congruently, and efficiently. Body language is not supposed to be some magic bullet that you use to get what you want from someone. It is suppose to be used to help you express what you want.

Common mistakes the Nice Guy makes with Dominance, Being in Control, and Leading

Another popular method many Nice Guys falsely believe will help then get better with expressing themselves is if they could learn how to be more dominant and aggressive. They want this not only when it come to getting women, but also in stopping the Jerk. As a result, many Nice Guys believe they always have to s be controlling with a woman, and maintain dominance of all of their interactions with her. This line of thought is understandable, in addition to the Conspiracy, there are numerous relationships and dating coaches and self-improvement gurus who say the man should be in control at all times.

Anyone who wants to constantly control something or someone, usually doesn't trust it or them, and/or is afraid of it or them. If you feel comfortable and relaxed with someone then you have no need to control them; you have peace of mind around them. You don't mind letting whatever happens happen, because you are not threatened by the outcome. You are open to the possibilities of the interaction. Nice Guys who feel an overwhelming need to dominate or control an interaction with a woman usually feel this because they are afraid. They are afraid because they do not believe they can handle the outcome of what they think is going to happen if they did not control it.

☢

This lack of trust usually comes from one of two places, either you don't trust what you will do, or you do not trust what she is going to do.

1. Lack of trust in yourself

Most Nice Guys do not trust themselves and this lack of trust, is the reason they want to control the situation or interaction. He is trying to hide the fact that he does not have enough confidence in what he is doing, or that he cannot handle the outcome.

There is nothing wrong with wanting to control the interaction if it is best for the situation. There is nothing wrong with insisting to lead if you truly are or believe your leadership is the best option for the two of you. It is not productive to want to be in control or lead the interaction because you are scared of appearing out of control, or because you are afraid of what you may do if you are not in charge and complete control. Wanting to lead for these reasons is not sincere, and people may resent you for it. They may resent you because you are being selfish, you are looking out for yourself at the expense of whoever you are trying to lead.

For example, it seems as if every year my friend "Tracy" decides he wants to become a vegetarian. Now every time he does this I am happy for him, but the problem is that every time he quits eating meat, he seems to forget that he is the one who wanted to give up meat, not me. It never failed, whenever we went out to eat, I knew I was in for a lecture on the evils of eating a nice juicy steak. My friends and I hated when he tried to tell us how to eat. I remember a time we were at a restaurant and he had the audacity to try to change our order for us. like we were his kids or something. I remember the moment things came to a boiling point.

We were at an afternoon cookout eating what most people eat at a cookout:meat. Tracy was going on and on and on about how bad meat was for us and I swear right before I was getting ready to give him a punch in his big mouth, I noticed something interesting. While he was ranting about the ills of eating meat yet again, I looked at his eyes and when I saw him looking at my plate full of delicious mouth-watering meat; I swear I saw lust in that man's eyes.

Then it hit me, he was not trying to convince us that eating meat was bad, he was trying to convince himself eating meat was bad. That was the moment when it became obvious to me that he was not trying to control us, or order our food for us because he was concerned about what we were eating. Tracy did not want the meat around because he was scared of what he was going to do. Deep inside he was not sure he could handle himself being around all that meat he wanted so badly, so he tried to control the one thing he thought he could control, us.

This is what many Nice Guys are doing when they are trying to control their interactions. They want to lead primarily because they do not think they can handle what the woman would do, or what they think is about to happen. They try to control her or the interaction via their own leadership. Their desire to lead is more about protecting themselves and/or getting what they want than it is about being best for the situation.

Other examples of Nice Guys trying to lead because of a lack of trust in self:

Changing conversation topics because he is afraid of appearing un-knowledgeable

Acting as if you know more about a situation than you actually do

Blaming or accusing her when you make a mistake in your leadership

Responding to situations disproportionately

Seeing all questions as challenges to your leadership

Trying to lead her so she will see you as a leader, because you do not think she will accept you otherwise

2. Lack of trust in others

This is where the Nice Guy wants to lead because he has a lack of trust in the person or persons he is dealing with to do what he think is right. Having your desire to lead be based on fear and mistrust of someone is a very dangerous and unhealthy reason to want to lead.

If the Nice Guy does not trust the other person to do the "right thing," or do what the Nice Guy wants them to do on their own, then they will often try to control them or they will try to always be around them. They want to be around them to "keep an eye" on them to make sure they are doing the "right thing." For example, look at security cameras in casinos, the casino bosses are watching the patrons as well as the employees. The bosses cannot and will not trust anyone around that much money. Now while this is understandable in a casino-employee, casino-boss relationship, it is dangerous behavior for a social and/or romantic relationship the Nice Guy is trying to manage.

This is where a lot of the snooping, following, and controlling behavior, comes from in relationships. A lot of Nice Guys exhibit this behavior because a Nice Guy may not trust the woman he is dating when she is out of his sight. He will do everything in his power not to let her out of his sight. I do not have to tell you how nonproductive a mindset this is to have for a relationship.

The issue with this is relatively easy to see. The only people who seem to have a hard time understanding this are the people who are in the middle of it.

Your desire to be in control with women or to lead a woman should not be based on a lack of trust in yourself or because you feel like you can't handle what she will say or do. You should earn the right to lead.

Earning the right to lead

The right to lead is mainly based on two things:

1. If you are the best option or most qualified to lead. People will follow someone if they feel safe, and if they believe they are in good hands, and they feel the person has a sense of what they are doing. The qualifications to lead can come in many different forms:

> Experience
>
> Physical Skill
>
> Knowledge
>
> Talent
>
> Expertise

2. If you have consent or permission to lead. Now what a lot of Nice Guys do not understand is that consent can come in many forms:

Verbal	Nonverbal
Conditional	Temporary
Mutual	Positional
Situational	Traditional
Seniority	Appointment
Implied	Voted

The hard part for most Nice Guys is to figure out which type of consent they have, or even if they have the consent to lead.

Now try to go back and remember all the times someone tried to control you, or tell you what to do, you were probably more offended than anything. This is because you could feel their desire to lead you was based on a lack of trust and/or fear. A major reason why things often go so badly for you when you try to lead or assert yourself, or act dominant out of fear or lack of trust, is because people can feel something is off. They know you are trying to be something that you are not, even if they cannot fully articulate what they are feeling to themselves or to you. You both know your leading/dominant behavior is not coming from a place that is genuine and/or is based on you trying to do right by those you are trying to lead. When you try to force control or leadership on someone, and/or when you come from a place where you are not the best option or genuine, disappointing results can often occur.

If you are not careful about the reason you are trying to lead, that is if your desire to lead comes from a selfish place, then you run the risk of coming across in a number of unflattering ways:

Selfish leadership can come across as:

Needy	Bossy
Desperate	Try-hard
Non-calibrated	Socially awkward
Unintelligent	Mean spirited
Angry	Pushy
Stubborn	Closed-minded
Inappropriate	Belligerent

When you are sincere with your intentions, and have whomever it is you are trying to lead best interests at heart, then you will have a much larger margin for error. That is because they know you are not being selfish, and making the interaction all about trying to please or protect you. Whomever you are trying to lead knows, at least subconsciously, that you are doing the best you can; they can feel you have their best interest at heart.

CHAPTER TEN

FRIEND ZONE

This section is devoted to the Friend Zone: what it is and what it isn't. This is a very important topic for the Nice Guy because this is where so many Nice Guys spend so much of their time. Now to manage your expectations, let it be known upfront, the purpose of this section is to examine the mindset of Nice Guys in the friend zone, as well as look at some of the issues that are specific to Nice Guys who are in the friend zone. This is so that you can be more efficient and effective in expressing yourself and using your Nice Guy tendencies while you are in the friend zone. This examination is not necessarily meant for you to get out of the friend zone so you can get her, this examination is meant to give you a different perspective on issues you may have had in the past regarding the friend zone. This examination is not meant to tell you what to do if you are in the friend zone with someone you want to be in a romantic/sexual relationship with.

What is the Friend Zone?

Let's define the friend zone. This is important because there are so many misconceptions about the friend zone. As far as Militant Nice Guy is concerned, the friend zone is any non-romantic and/or nonsexual interactions men have with a female.

There is nothing inherently wrong with being in the friend zone. What most Nice Guys do not understand is there are two different groups of guys in the friend zone: guys who want to be there, and guys who do not. One group has given the term "friend zone" a bad name, because they are loud and vocal about their dissatisfaction about being in there.

In the first group, you have the guys who actually want to be in the friend zone. They are totally happy being there and only want a platonic non-romantic and nonsexual relationship with the woman. They are content to be in the friend zone because they chose or want to be there.

Then there is the second group who gives being in the friend zone a bad name. These Nice Guys are not happy to be in the friend zone usually because they want more from the friendship than the friend zone can give them, and they are frustrated. This is because it is frustrating when you want to be in a romantic relationship with someone and they only want to be "just friends."

Phrases women use to keep Nice Guys in the friend zone:

But I see you as a brother

You are such a good friend

It's not you; it's me

I don't see you in that way

I do not want to ruin what we have

I trust you too much to be with you

You are too important to me as a friend to take that risk

Many women have used these phrases and many more like them to keep Nice Guys in the friend zone and frustrated. I think it would benefit us if we were to take quick look at some of the ways we get in the friend zone in the first place.

Common actions that put Nice Guy in the friend zone:

Waiting for the right time to be romantic.
(There is no right time to be romantic. The best time be romantic is when you feel it.)

Not interacting with her romantically/sexually.
(Sex and/or sexual tension is the number thing that separates romantic relationships from platonic ones)

Not telling her you want more from her.
(Women are not mind readers. How else is she going to know you want more if you do not tell her?)

Being afraid of telling her what you want.
(Try figuring out why you are afraid and then proceed accordingly.)
Not being sure about what you want from her.

(If you do not know what you want from her, then how do you know you don't belong in the friend zone?)

Waiting on her to make the first move.
(What if she was waiting on you to make the first move?)

These are among the many reason why so many Nice Guys get stuck in the friend zone accidentally. Now there are several methods, and tactics, and strategies that exist already to get Nice Guys out of the friend zone, many Nice Guys have heard about some of these methods or tried some of the following:

Eliminate contact for a while

Try to be more flirty or sexual

Be more dominant or masculine

Tease her

Try to be more like the Jerk

Make her jealous with another woman

Now these methods may all work to different degrees of success, however. for the most part they do not work. Most Nice Guys who have tried them continue to stay stuck in the friend zone. There is nothing wrong with you, the problem is not with you, but with your advice. Traditional Nice Guy advice for getting out of the friend zone is often only meant to work in a vacuum, that is. if only the two of you existed in a world all to yourselves.

We don't live in a vacuum, we live in a world with Jerks. The other major reason why traditional Nice Guy advice is often ineffective is because it does not take into account the Jerk with his superior strategic advantage. How many times have you been interacting with a woman, being considerate and respectful, and a Jerk just shows up out of the blue and takes her from you? Before you know it, you are in the friend zone.

If you know Jerks are out there, one of the best ways you can deal with them more efficiently is to learn from your mistakes so you will not make them anymore (or at least make fewer of them). That is why we are going to focus on some common mistakes that Nice Guys make when trying to get out of the friend zone.

Do You Deserve to Get Out of the Friend Zone?

A big reason why Nice Guys find it difficult to get out of the friend zone is because many Nice Guys have the wrong motivation. One reason why most tactics to get out of the friend zone do not work or are difficult to pull off is because often, the Nice Guy does not deserve to get out of the friend zone. Just because you want to get out of the friend zone does not automatically mean that you should. You should have a reason beyond your desire to get out.

What you must do is ask yourself, Why do I want out of the friend zone? What is my motivation for pushing this woman to be in a relationship with me?. Many Nice Guys have the wrong motivation for wanting to move out of the friend zone. The woman can sense that your motivation is not genuine, and that may be why she is rejecting your offer. You truly deserve to get out of the friend zone if you are doing it for the right reasons. The truth of the matter is that many Nice Guys who want to get out of the friend zone want to do so for selfish reasons.

Some of the most common selfish reasons for Nice Guys wanting out of the friend zone:

Sex

You want to have sex and she is your only sexual option. Or, you are sexually attracted to her, and you want to be in a relationship with her so you can have sex with her. Your desire to get out of the friend zone is not based on a romantic relationship being the best option for the both of you, but to satisfy your desire for sex.

Jealously

She is having sex with someone else who you do not think is good enough for her. Or, you may be jealous of the relationship the other guy has with her, and you want that relationship with her for yourself. Your motivation for being with her romantically is more about you trying to take her from the other guy than it is about being with her because that is what you honestly think is best for the two of you.

Loneliness

You are lonely and want companionship, and she is your only option. Your thinking, I might as well, make her my woman, she is here and I am lonely, so why not? Your main motivation to be with her is based on your lack of options, as opposed to anything else. This is more about you curing your loneliness than it is about doing what is best for the relationship.

Obligation

You feel she owes you a relationship because of something you did for her. Your desire is quid pro quo based, I give you something, and then you give me a relationship. The desire to be in a romantic relationship is based on exchange, and not what is best for her.

Ambition

You want to prove to yourself that you could get her. For example: The guy who wants to date a model, so he can prove how cool he is to others. He only wants to be with her to take value from the woman and/ or he is using her to improve his status. His desire to be with her is not about genuine attraction, it is more about, Look at me and what I did; I must be special, or a somebody because I got her.

Often, when a woman rejects your offer to take things to another level, she is justified. This is because she may know that you are being selfish, and/or you are only thinking about yourself and your feelings. And this is not a good enough reason for her to get involved in a romantic/sexual relationship with you. The optimal reason you should want to get out of the friend zone is because getting out of the friend zone is the best option for the both of you.

Always be closing

There are those who say that the best way to get out of the friend zone is to never get stuck in the friend zone in the first place. They say you should never hesitate and to always express attraction and interest as soon as you see a woman you think you might have even a chance of being in a relationship with her.

If you were to listen to the Conspiracy, then it would have you to believe it is your fault that you are always getting stuck in the friend zone. It is the Conspiracy that makes you feel as if your hesitation is a bad thing. It is what makes you feel that you are not man enough or that something is wrong with you for the times that you hesitate when you see something you might want. You have no doubt heard some variation of the phrases: go after what you want, always express yourself. Women love a man of action.

First of all, if you want to be genuine, then you should express interest or desire for a woman because you genuinely feel it for her. Your desire for expressing attraction for her should not be based on your fear of getting stuck in the friend zone. Second, those who advocate you should just be a man, and always, immediately express attraction and escalate, often have a limited view of how genuine attraction works for a Nice Guy.

For many Nice Guys, being attracted to women in general is similar to being attracted to music in general. There are some songs you like the first time you hear them, some grow on you, some you hate at first and then come to love them, and so forth and so on. That is how genuine attraction works for the majority of Nice Guys. Nice Guys are attracted to what they are interested in and sometimes that is not immediately apparent or clear at the time. Because Nice Guys are looking for a genuine attraction, simply expressing attraction for the sake of doing is not usually an option for the Nice Guy.

This is the major paradox with expressing attraction for attraction's sake. Either you are faking it and she can sense this through all of your smooth lines and that turns her off. Or, you succeeded in tricking her into thinking you were attracted to her, but because you were being insincere, you do not respect and appreciate her attraction to you. This is because your interaction is based on a lie, and for many Nice Guys, this is a turn-off.

Expressing attraction just to do it often works, but at what cost to you? Most Nice Guys are not willing to sell themselves out like that. Most Nice Guys want to be sure before they express their attraction because they want their expression of it to be genuine.

Many Nice Guys want to be sure and sincere so they hesitate to be certain they are sure. The problem is because of his consideration of her feelings, and his own processing of his emotions, Nice Guys are often placed in the friend zone. By the time he knows how she feels all figured out, and how he wants to be with her, and is ready put together a plan of action, it is too late.

Far too many Nice Guys mistake their hesitation for weakness, or for being indecisive. Most Nice Guys do not realize this contemplation process is a very important part of how they go about being certain they are sure and sincere in what they are about to do. This is because he is conscious and considerate of how his actions may affect her. Nice Guys would do themselves a tremendous favor if they taught themselves how to look at their hesitation as processing.

The reason why hesitating has such a bad reputation is because Nice Guys do not fundamentally know why they are hesitating, and they do not even know if the reasons for hesitating are valid. This is because they have little or no experience trusting themselves and their reasons for hesitating. This lack of trust makes Nice Guys feel uncertain, and Nice Guys confuse this uncertainty with weakness. As far as this book is concerned, any reason to hesitate is valid as long as it is legitimate and sincere.

There is nothing wrong with hesitating, so long as you are aware that you are doing it. And, as long as you know the tremendous disadvantage that results from hesitating and/or processing. Much of the frustration

Nice Guys experience when processing is because they think they will be rewarded for their consideration. The sooner Nice Guys understand and accept what position their caring and consideration puts them in tactically, especially in relation to the Jerk, the better position they will be in to deal with her and the Jerk. The Conspiracy has told you to never hesitate, they view it as a sign of weakness. All hesitation means is that you are unsure of how to proceed, that is it. Is does not make you weak, it is not a character flaw.

Probing

Another major mistake Nice Guy's make when trying to get out of the friend zone is probing. Probing is any action, method, or activity that is meant to figure out how she feels about you so you can know how to feel about her, and/or how to proceed.

The way probing works is like this: Let's say you were talking to a woman you were interested in and she asked you if you were attracted to her or not. Now let's say your response to her was, "Well first tell me how do you feel about me?" This would be an example of probing, because you are trying to find out how she feels about you so you would know how to respond to her question. If she says that she likes you, then you will proceed to tell her that you like her. If she says that she does not like you, and as a result of her response, you then either tell her that you do not like her, or you will say nothing.

The problem with probing is your reason for asking your question is not sincere. You are asking her if she likes you under the disguise of getting information from her, which is not your real reason. The real reason you are asking her how she feels is because you are unsure of how to proceed. What you are doing is using her to tell you what to say and do next. Probing is nonproductive because in this case, you really are interested in her, but you are afraid to say so, that is why you want her to answer you first.

In essence, what you are doing is making her responsible for determining the direction of the interaction or relationship. Often, women can feel that pressure. You are forcing her to make the first move.

Furthermore, you are giving her this responsibility without her consent, or approval. If you are not careful, she may even resent you a little for it. You made her responsible with moving the relationship forward not because you think that is what is best, but you made it based on fear, because you do not want to make the decision yourself to move the relationship forward.

When she's ready to move the relationship forward, she will let you know in her own time. If you want to ask her how she feels to see if her feelings match yours, to see if you two are on the same page, that is fine. However, probing so you can use her answer to determine how you feel about her, shows a lack of integrity.

Probing to find out how she feels so that you can know how to answer her question is not the behavior of someone who knows and is proud of how they feel. If you know how you feel, and are proud of your feelings, then you would not want or need to ask her how she feels about you first. It should make no difference to you whatsoever how she feels about you if you are answering her question proudly and honestly.

☢

Tell me now

This is a classic mistake the Nice Guy makes when he is trying to get out of the friend zone. This is where the Nice Guy has worked up the courage and decided to talk to her about getting out of the friend zone and into a relationship with him. He sees this moment as a big deal for him and, as his moment of truth. This is usually a pressure-filled moment for the Nice Guy where he expresses how he feels and waits for a response from her.

Here is the thought process for how many Nice Guys get to the point of where they are finally ready to ask her to be more than just friends: Wow this woman is really amazing. Do I like her? Yea, I think I like her. I think I am going to try to be with her. But how will me asking her to be more than what we are affect the friendship? I don't know what to do, but I do like her though. I think I am going to talk to her about this. No I should not. Yea I think I should. No I should not. Oh to hell with it, I think I will tell her how I feel.

So what does he do, he decides to tell her how he feels, and then he sits there and waits for her answer. More often than not, she will not have one. Now a common mistake some Nice Guys make is to confuse her silence or non-answer with rejection. The main reason Nice Guys do this is because they are going into the talk with her expecting her to answer to his question, and not purely making the discussion about expressing how he feels about her.

The major issue the "tell me now" mindset, is he was not only telling her how he felt, because that is how he was feeling, but he was also telling her how he felt because he was looking for a particular response from her. She did not respond the way he wanted and he was disappointed. This disappointment with him not getting the answer he wanted can lead to feelings of insecurity and frustration. What most Nice Guys do is try to get her to fix this is by trying to insist that she to give him an answer at that particular moment.

Here is something most people do not know about the "tell me now mindset." If you make her choose right then and there, between being with you, and being "just friends," she will more than likely choose to be "just friends." What is difficult for many Nice Guys to understand is even if she was considering being with you and you asked her for your answer right then and there, she will more than likely choose the friends route. Most people if they have to choose between the known or the unknown will choose the known. And if you are asking her to choose between your continued friendship or between a romantic relationship with you, then she will more than likely make the "safe" decision and choose the friendship. This is mainly because you did not give her a chance to go through the same thought process you went through to get to the same point you did.

This point reminds me of a time when I got into a heated argument with my friend "Beth." We had a disagreement over the time when our mutual friend, "Monica," told Beth about what happened after she told her boyfriend Eric she was pregnant, and the boyfriend got upset. Beth's immediate knee-jerk reaction was to call Eric a pig. I said to Beth, "I do not understand why she thinks Eric is a pig." She said Eric should be happy Monica is pregnant, and this is great news for the couple.

I asked her, "How is Eric suppose know that?" I told her, "I bet when Monica found out that she was pregnant, she freaked out at first. It probably took her a while to analyze what the baby would mean to her life.

She probably had to take time to figure out what she was going to do. I know she probably talked to at least one person about the news to give her a sounding board."

Now Eric, who has just gotten the news that his girlfriend is pregnant, has to process the information in seconds and is expected come to the same conclusion as Monica. That was not fair to Eric. Monica had a chance to be upset, so why not Eric? The issue was not necessarily Eric being upset at the news that Monica is pregnant, the issue is that she was taking away Eric's chance to think and process the information he just received. If he is pressed to express how he feels on the spot, then of course he is going to be upset.

What Monica could have done in this situation is what Nice Guys could try, that is to give him a chance to let the information to sink in, to let him absorb and process the full weight of what was said to him. A non-answer is not necessarily a no, but it can feel like one, especially to Nice Guys who went into the talk wanting an answer right then. In many cases, time is the key to dealing with the non-answer. If you get the sense that they are hesitating or need time, you can either give them some time to respond, or ask them if they would like some time to respond.

Tell me more

Tell me more is the cousin to the non-answer. Nice Guys often confuse any response that is not a yes as a rejection. They think she is saying no to them when often that is not the case, what she could really be saying is, "Tell me more." When the Nice Guy asks her to be more that just friends the woman will often respond with a variation on the following phrases:

I do not want to ruin what we have

Do you really see the two of us together

What about what my ex boyfriend

I don't think it will work

Or she may just sit there

142

Many Nice Guys will mistakenly misinterpret these statements as rejections.

When she is saying I do not want to ruin what we have, she is not necessarily saying no, I do not want to be with you. What she could be saying is, tell me your plan for us.

When she is saying, "Do you really see the two of us together?" She could be saying, "We are two completely different people, do you really think we would be a good fit together?"

When she asks, "What about my ex boyfriend?" that could mean, "How do you plan to handle him, he's crazy?"

If she is saying, "I do not think this will work," what she could be saying is, "Tell me why you think it will work?"

If she just sits there, she may be thinking, I haven't even thought about the two of us being together, I need a moment.

Nice Guys are often so preoccupied with looking for a yes to their question, and on avoiding rejection, until they often miss an excellent opportunity to address concerns she may have about moving out of the friend zone and getting into a romantic relationship with him.

Asking a woman to get into a relationship with you is like asking someone to invest in you. And people are very reluctant to invest in someone without a very good reason or reasons. Unless you tell her why you think being with you is a good thing, you will have a hard time getting to see things your way.

Getting her through gratitude

Another mistake the Nice Guy makes when trying to get out of the friend zone is trying to get her through gratitude. The Nice Guy often believes if he can do enough things for her, then she will be grateful, and as a result of her gratitude she will like him more.

Now there are those who believe trying to get a woman's gratitude is wrong, they see doing anything for a woman as supplication. There are even those who will go so far as to advocate never doing anything for a woman or that helping women with their problems is for her girlfriends and not for men.

Well many Nice Guys find this type of thinking troubling because, part of caring about someone is helping them with their problems. Whether the Nice Guy was trying to move out of the friend zone or not, most Nice Guys are genuinely concerned with the woman with whom he is friends. When Nice Guys are friends with someone they want to help them with their problems, this even includes problems she may have with getting over another guy. Too many Nice Guys have been made to feel bad for trying to help someone they care about. The Nice Guy is not doing anything wrong in that aspect, she is/was his friend and she wanted his help, and he wants to help her.

This help could come in many forms, it could include anything from: doing favors for her, helping her out of a tough financial situation, helping her study for a test, to helping her to get over a bad relationship etc.

Often, when a Nice Guy succeeds in helping a woman, she will express her gratitude to him. Nice Guys often mistake this gratitude for attraction and/or sexual interest. As a result, he mistakenly thinks he is either making progress towards a relationship and/or sex, or he thinks that he is in a much better position with her than is the reality. Many Nice Guys falsely believe that if they help her with her problems, then she will reward him with a relationship, and/or sex. Attraction does not work this way.

Gratitude does not automatically equal an increase in romantic or sexual interest. She will often see your doing a favor or favors for her as simply being part of your duty and/or role as being her friend. Her gratitude or appreciation of what you did for her is not necessarily a sign that you are making progress toward a romantic\sexual relationship; it is merely her showing her appreciation for you doing your job as a friend

This is not to say that gratitude does not sometimes lead to a woman seeing you in a different light, or that it won't lead to a romantic relationship. This is only to say using gratitude as a way to get her is not a good plan to get out of the friend zone for three main reasons:

1. Gratitude is not practical

Getting her through gratitude is not practical because attraction does not work this way. Attraction is not systematic, it is not the result of a series of steps, the getting attraction via gratitude approach is far too logic based. If gratitude systematically led to attraction then many more women would be in romantic relationships and/or having sex with Nice Guys. Nice Guys are notorious for doing whatever women want. Many Nice Guys have done the following: homework; covered shifts at work; paid rent; talked on the phone about some Jerk for hours; dropped whatever they were doing for her; and so much more. All to watch her run off and have a relationship/sex with some Jerk who did not do any of this for her.

This is a major reason why so many Nice Guys lose many of their women to Jerks who she has known far shorter time than she has known the Nice Guy. This is because the Nice Guy spent all of his time doing stuff for her, and the Jerk spent his time with her trying to have sex with her.

For example, if you were to take her to an expensive concert then more than likely, she would be grateful to you, this is how most people feel when you do something nice for them. There is nothing wrong with taking her to the concert if all you want was her gratitude and for her to have a great time. However, if you were taking her to the concert and you expected part of her gratitude to include sex with her, only because you took her to the concert then you will probably have a problem with that expectation. This is not necessarily because she does not want to have sex with you, it is just that you did nothing during the concert to express your desire or interest in her.

If she is at the concert with you, then there is a strong possibility that she could be interested in you, and she is grateful to you because you invited her to the concert. However, the mistake many Nice Guys make in these types of situations is not doing anything to let her know how you feel about her. The Nice Guy often relies on the fact that he asked her out, or the concert to do the job of expressing how he feels and what he wants for them. He thinks, Well, she should know I like her and want something serious because I asked her to the concert. Expressing how you feel is your job, not the concert's job. A woman's gratitude is not going to make her want to have a relationship or sex with you in and of itself, especially if the desire was not there in the first place. The best you can expect from gratitude is to put you in a better position to express how you feel about her.

2. Gratitude does not necessarily change how someone sees you.

Her gratitude is only an indicator of her appreciating the person she thinks you are already. For example, if she needs to borrow a thousand dollars, her feelings of gratitude for whoever gives her the money will not change how she fundamentally feels about the person giving the money to her. Her getting the money from either her Nice Guy coworker, her guy friend who wants to have sex with her, the funny guy at the gym, or her smart salsa instructor, does not change how she feels fundamentally about those guys.

Her coworker will still be just the Nice Guy coworker; the guy friend will still be just the horny guy she will not have sex with; the guy at the gym will still be just a funny guy; her salsa instructor will still be just her smart salsa instructor. Her gratitude for any one of those guys giving her money will not necessarily, fundamentally change how she feels about him.

3. You are not being genuine

Seeking her gratitude because you think it will lead to you getting what you want from her is not genuine. There is nothing wrong with wanting to help someone because you care about them and you want to help them out. There is also nothing wrong with you helping her for her gratitude in and of itself.

However, too many guys try to bribe her into compliance by doing something for her. They have a, "If I do this for you, then you will do this for me" mindset. Or, "If I do this for her, then she will like me more," mindset. This is ineffective because you are using her gratitude as a means to get something else from her. When her gratitude does come, you will be disappointed because you did not get what you were looking for beyond her gratitude. This can lead to eventual disappointment and/or frustration.

This is because you expected more from your gratitude than it was ever meant to do. Most Nice Guys do not understand the limits of gratitude. When you understand what gratitude can and cannot do for getting you out of the friend zone then you will be able to use it properly.

How Nice Guys Let Jerks Dominate Their Relationships with Women

Most Nice Guys have had to deal with some variation of the all too familiar scenario of helping a woman they want get over some Jerk or a bad relationship. Most Nice Guys usually help women get over Jerks for a combination of the following reasons:

They genuinely care about her

They think they are better for her than he is

They want him out of her life

They are jealous

They want help her to move on

But what usually happens is either she doesn't move on and she stays with the Jerk, or she breaks up with him and moves on to another Jerk just like him. And she almost never decides to get with the Nice Guy who was there for her and helped her to get over the Jerk in the first place. We all have spent countless hours wondering, What the hell happened? Why doesn't she see just how good I am for her, and how did me helping her to get over someone else who was treating her so poorly land me in the friend zone again?

The issue for most Nice Guys in this situation is, How did this starting out as one friend trying to help out another turn me into her personal therapist? Now, the way this normally works is somehow during the course of you trying to help her to get over the Jerk, somehow your every conversation with the woman slowly became all about this Jerk and what he is or is not doing. She eventually starts calling you morning, noon and night to talk about this guy. It seem the more she talks to you about him, the more she wants to talk to you about him, and this frustrates you because you know you have become a therapist.

The problem is not necessarily you helping her to move on, but the problem is letting her problems with the Jerk dominate your every conversation with her. When you let her go on and on about this guy, what you are doing is training her to come to you to talk about him. Your conversations all start to become about him, while the Jerk becomes a major reason why she is talking to you. This is how the Jerk comes to dominate your interactions with her and turns you from potential boyfriend into therapist.

A few signs to tell if the Jerk is dominating your relationship with a woman:

Every time you two talk his name comes up

He is the first topic of conversation

She moves the conversation back to him, every time you move the conversation off him

You are sick of hearing about him

You feel obligated to talk about him

You consistently feel somewhat frustrated when you are done talking to her about him

When you are constantly talking to her about him you are in danger of making the Jerk the driving force of your relationship. Talking about him becomes familiar not only to her, but to you to. You are in extreme danger of his actions affecting your well-being also. You might start to think about him and his actions even when you are not talking to her about him. If it gets really bad, then you could also become one of the reasons why she has a hard time getting over him. This is because you two now have some kind of weird emotional threesome happening.

When you let the Jerk be the main focus of your conversations, then you leave no room for you to talk about yourself. If you truly believe that you are the better option, then it would be advisable for you not to spend so much time talking to her about the inferior option. If you do not talk about who you are and what you want, then who will?

When the Jerk is interacting with her, do you think he talks to her about you as much as you talk about him? Do you think he talks about you at all? Is he as focused on you as you are on him? If the Jerk is dominating your conversations with the woman, then all you are doing is helping keep the Jerk on her mind. What do you think is best for the woman, you talking to her hours on end about getting over some Jerk? How about being the reason she has gotten over the Jerk? If you think you are best option for her, and if you believe that she is better off with you, then you owe it to yourself, and her, to declare yourself, and make your intentions clear.

Most Nice Guys' difficulty in getting out of the friend zone is usually the result of them picking an inefficient/ineffective way of going about getting what they want. Failure to get out of the friend zone does not automatically prove there is something wrong with who you are and what you want.

CHAPTER ELEVEN

SEX

What is sex?

The best way to describe what this section is to describe what it is not. Even though this section is about sex, it is not about the physical act of sex itself. Also, this section is not about how to get women in bed with you, (there is already a ton of information in books, on radio, on television, on the internet, etc., which can help you with that pursuit). Nor is this section judging whether sex is a good thing or bad thing, or assigning any moral value to sex.

This section is about examining how the Conspiracy's manipulation of the Nice Guy's self-esteem has influenced his view toward sex. It also discusses how this view affects the Nice Guy in the pursuit of sex, and how he expresses himself sexually. This is about examining how the Nice Guy sees sex, with the goal of making him more effective in expressing his sexuality. Effective sexual expression is the Nice Guy's best weapon in the war to stop the more focused and better equipped Jerk from undeservedly having sex with the woman you are perusing and/or are involved with. The first thing we need to understand is how to become more efficient at expressing sexual desire and to understand how the Nice Guy views sex.

Effective sexual expression is important to the Nice Guy because if you are ineffective in asking for and/or getting sex, then simply put, you will not have it. If you do not have sex, or can't have sex, then your lack of success will make it all too easy for you to become overly preoccupied with getting sex. Because of this, your sexual desire or frustration will begin to control you. In other words, the less sex you get, the less effective you will be at getting it. This is because you lack the ability and the experience to act on your sexual desires. Ironically, this lack of success with sex can make you even hornier and more determined to get sex, often making you even less effective, it is a vicious cycle.

Your sexual desire will create an aura of horniness and desperation, which will affect your interactions with women. Women will find this unattractive and off-putting because your sexual desire is not appropriate to the situation. Or, is it impersonal, meaning that you see her primarily as an object to satisfy your horniness. Women do not mind sexual appreciation as long as it is appropriate to the situation. Women want to feel that you have control over your sexual desires, not that your sexual desires have control over you.

Women, Jerks, and Sex

When it comes to getting time, attention, and respect from a woman, there is one thing to keep in mind for Nice Guys: Generally, he who has sex with her first wins. A Nice Guy could have spent every Monday night through Friday night with a woman he cares about curled up on the sofa, watching movies with her until two in the morning for six months. All that time he spent with her does not matter if he did not have sex with her when it comes to who she makes a priority in her life.

☢

When it comes to who has the prime position in a woman's life, sex is a major determining factor, it does not matter if:

You gave her money

Gave her kids money

Put her through school

Was there for her

Cuddle with her on the weekends

Have a connection

Would die for her

Would kill for her

If her friends and family like you

Why does it not matter? Because, if this woman (who the Nice Guy wants so bad) were to meet a no good, clearly bad for her Jerk on the Sunday between their sexless get-togethers, and has sex with him then he moves past the Nice Guy in her hierarchy of who has a priority in her life. Countless Nice Guys have experienced their time, effort, and energy rendered null and void to a woman who they have invested in, once she has sex with some other guy, especially a Jerk.

Sex to a woman is very important and most women try not to take that responsibility lightly. This is part of the reason why she moves those Jerks ahead of you. Making him the top priority is very important in her mind because she just had sex with him. In her mind, she gave him something valuable (a gift) and she doesn't want to appear as if she has given away that gift lightly, to herself, or to him. For her to have sex (give her gift away) to just anyone, would reflect poorly on her decision making process in her mind. This is a major reason why many times she moves someone who is undeserving ahead of you.

Many Nice Guys have lost so much sleep wondering how and why women keep having sex with Jerk after Jerk.. How can she keep falling for the same crap over and over? This is because many times, in her mind, she was not tricked or manipulated. One thing about being manipulated is most people do not even know when it is happening to them. It seems once a woman has sexually invested in the Jerk, then it becomes hard for her to let him go.

Many women feel there is rarely a greater investment a woman can make in a guy than for her to have sex with him. It is almost as if after she has sex, she loses the ability to tell that the Jerk is not good for her, or is manipulating her. She could have met him wearing an orange jumpsuit covered in blood, but if she has sex with him then boom he moves to the head of the line (ahead of you). She will start to rationalize, Well maybe he isn't so bad after all. Her rational for this is often based on the fact that she had sex with him.

If she doesn't move him ahead of you, and every guy in her life she is not having sex with, then what does that say about her decision making process? It is in large part how she justifies to herself why she chose the Jerk over the Nice Guy. It does not matter if he does not deserve the top spot, as far as she is concerned he is the priority.

History is full of Nice Guys like you who can testify to the power of Jerks. They cannot be stopped, the best thing we can do as Nice Guys is work on ourselves, and become more efficient at expressing ourselves sexually. To help you to become more efficient and effective, let's look at the sexual stigma, and its effect on the Nice Guy.

☢

The sexual stigma and its effect on the Nice Guy

Another major reason why Nice Guys are at a disadvantage sexually is because the average Nice Guy, for the most part, has dualistic view when it comes to sex. On one hand, Nice Guys see the act of sex as something beautiful, which is meant to be shared with someone who they think is special. And on the other hand, Nice Guys see sex as something dirty done in the dark by sluts and bad people. Most Nice Guys tend to put women into two categories sexually: the ones you just have sex with; these women are whores, sluts, and tramps. And then there are the ones you marry, the good girls, angels, and fun girls. There is very little overlap between the two. It is the classic case of Madonna-Whore complex. It is the dualistic way Nice Guys see women where they only see women as either a good-girl or a bad-girl, a virgin or a slut.

☢

The Jerk and the Sexual Stigma

Now Jerks generally place any woman they are attracted to sexually into the slut category. It does not matter if she caused his attraction on purpose, or by accident. It does not matter if she even wants his attention or not, it does not even matter if she is even aware of it. This objectification is very important to the Jerk because this is what allows him to do what most Nice Guy can't. This objectification is a big part of what allows the Jerk to be able to use and get what he wants from the woman and to feel very little guilt and regret, if any, afterwards.

The Jerk, after he has used her sexually, will often not feel any remorse because he sees her as a slut who deserves to be used. Ironically, usually the way she gets to be seen as a slut by the Jerk is either by him wanting to have sex with her, or by her actually having sex with him. Most of the time even if they do not have sex, he will still see her as a slut. To him, she will simply be a slut who hasn't had sex with him yet. This overly simplified view of women and sex is how he justifies his actions, "Oh she is just a whore she deserves it." He has to see her as a slut because if he saw her as a person who was worthy of respect and consideration, and then degraded her, or used her, then what would that say about him.

Women and the Sexual Stigma

In this society/culture, many women have as hard of a time navigating the virgin-slut dynamic as do Nice Guys. The reason why these women have such a hard time navigating this dynamic is because while women want to be seen as sexual, they do not want to be seen as sluts or promiscuous. The problem for women (and for Nice Guys) is there is no standard agreed upon definition for what constitutes a slut. The reason why women have such a hard time navigating their sexual world is because the standards for how she is suppose to behave sexually are ill-defined, poorly formed, fickle, and most importantly, open to interpretation. What all of this has done in part is to create massive confusion for how female sexuality is to be interpreted and is expressed.

For example, when does the following go from appropriate female sexual behavior any woman would engage in to slutty behavior?

If she had sex with five guys in:

Her life

Five years

This year

The past six months

The past month

The past two weeks

The past week

Twenty-four hours

No one can say for sure, the line is murky at best. Most women do not know where the line between slutty and sexy is, and this vagueness has caused many women, and men, to be uncertain as to just what are the standards?. Now what this uncertainty has done to women is constantly put them on edge about what is acceptable sexual behavior. Women are fearful of being judged poorly for their sexual behavior and/or choices. Her navigation of the sexual stigma is further complicated because she also has to be on the lookout for Jerks who are only interested in her sexually and the other potential consequences of sex: pregnancy, STDs, damaging her reputation, misinterpretations and/or misunderstandings after sex etc.

Most Nice Guys are aware of this sexual stigma, and they are sensitive to it. Many of the problems a Nice Guy may have with perusing sex with a woman may come from how he navigates dealing with this sexual stigma.

Understanding the sexual stigma is important because it looms over many of the decisions the Nice Guy makes when it comes to how he pursues sex with women. A big part of many of the Nice Guy's difficulty in his sexual pursuit of women is because he is hampered by his desire of not wanting the woman to feel insulted or disrespected by his sexual desire for her.

This is one of the most important reasons the Nice Guy is hesitant to express sexual interest in a women. He is interested in this because he cares about her well-being, and he wants to make sure the woman he wants clearly understands what his intentions are towards her. Because he is aware of the stigma often associated with sex, most Nice Guys want to reassure his woman that he is not some Jerk trying to use her for sex. This desire, coupled with there not being any hard and fast rules about what is appropriate sexual conduct, makes the Nice Guy unsure of himself. Often a Nice Guy confuses his totally natural and understandable uncertainty with how he should proceed sexually with a woman may think that he is weak or flawed.

There are a number of theories floating around as to why guys only put women in either the virgin/slut category. The reasons why guys think in this dualistic view, is not nearly as important as understanding the limits of this type of thinking. The major flaw of the virgin/slut, dynamic is that it does not take into account the messy realities of real life. This dynamic forces Nice Guys to see women as either a virgin or a slut, with no place for where the vast majority of women exist, somewhere between extremes of the virgin/slut dynamic.

Most Nice Guys know the woman they are interested in more than likely has a sexual past. Most Nice Guys accept her sexuality and sexual past, and believe that by her having a sexual past, that in and of itself, does not automatically make her a slut.

The main question we should ask ourselves is: Why are Nice Guys using the virgin/slut dynamic to guide their sexual pursuit in the first place? The virgin/slut is an inefficient, imperfect, impractical system that only works in the most extreme and/or theoretical cases when it comes to interacting with women.

A major mistake many Nice Guys make with the virgin/slut dynamic is using that as a guide to help him determine how he should feel about her, and how he should proceed, and behave around her. The virgin/slut dynamic distracts the Nice Guy from determining for himself how he should best proceed, and from him determining on his own why he wants her. He should be focused on his own reason, and not some impractical, imperfect, arbitrary guide like the virgin/slut dynamic.

If you are not careful, the dualistic nature of the virgin/slut dynamic will force you to see the woman as either a virgin or a slut, and not how she really is and how she relates to you. It forces you to abandon your thoughts, feelings, and emotions, towards her and adopts someone else's. Because of the duality of the virgin/slut dynamic, the Nice Guy will have a hard time paying attention to her individual sexuality, and to his particular situation.

The virgin/slut dynamic does not allow him to meet her where she is in the moment. It forces him to put her someplace where she may not exist. This is a major reason why the Nice Guy is ineffective in expressing his sexual interest. Taking the virgin/slut point of view will cause the Nice Guy to filter all of his sexual expression through this dynamic and not through his genuine sexual desire. Weather she is a virgin or slut should be irrelevant to your desires and how you treat her.

How Nice Guys Dilute Their Sexual Power

If you were to ask a Nice Guy why he likes the woman he likes, more often than not, he will give you a whole list of reasons why he is into her, beyond her sexuality.

Some reasons Nice Guys are attracted to women other than sexually:
Personality
Style
Sense of humor
Her sweetness
Intelligence
Strong personality
Ease of conversation

The problem with caring about the whole woman in addition to her sexuality is that it distracts you from the pursuit of sex. Anything that distracts you from the pursuit of sex is bad for your sex life. Even if these distractions are important to you, important to her, relevant, and/or necessary to how you chose to interact with her. Do not mistake this explanation of Nice Guys diluting their sexual power as an indictment against liking/appreciating the non sexual aspects of her. Militant Nice Guy is looking at this from a purely logistical/tactical perspective. Understanding how you are diluting your sexual power is important because most Nice Guys do not even realize this is even happening.

As a result of the Nice Guy caring and being interested in the whole woman, he does not make sex his number one priority; although it is still a major one. Because of this, he is at a sexual disadvantage, because caring and being interested in the whole woman diminishes his ability to pursue sex effectively.

Sex to the Nice Guy is very important; it is just that it is often not his number one priority. Unfortunately for him, many times in the process of him getting to know and enjoying the whole woman, his sexual pursuit of her often gets pushed down his list of priorities. This is not productive especially when he is in competition with some Jerk who is only interested in the woman sexually. Because of his sexual disadvantage, the Nice Guy has to do a much better job of expressing his sexual desire to compensate.

One way is to understand that a major problem with total appreciation is that often women cannot see things from the Nice Guy's point of view. Because most women do not understand or recognize his total appreciation of her as a result, most women cannot properly appreciate what it is that he is doing for her and how he feels about all of her. Ironically, many women will misread the Nice Guy's total enjoyment of her and many of his actions will be misinterpreted.

☢

Women often mistake a Nice Guys' total appreciation of her for:
Weakness
Indecisiveness
Non interest in her
Fear
Uncertainty
Not knowing what to do

So many women are so used to being pursued only sexually until they often mistake any other type of interest in her as non-romantic/non-sexual interest. This is a major reason why it would benefit you as a Nice Guy to make sexual expression more of a priority when interacting with a woman who whom you are interested. This is because your sexual interest in her is in competition with the other interest that you have in her. This is often why women think Nice Guys are not as expressive sexually as Jerks, because their sexual desire for her is in competition with their other interest in her. Express your genuine sexual desire.

How the Nice Guy's Caring Affects his Sexual Expression

What the Conspiracy has done is brilliant. They have taken the natural processing that you go through or have when you are considering having sex and turned it against you, by making you feel like this is a bad thing. Unfortunately, most Nice Guys can recall numerous times when they felt like they were not man enough or masculine enough. This may be because they had interactions with women where they were not one hundred percent sure of everything, or he had everything all figured out regarding how he feels about her and how he want to proceed especially sexually.

Some of the more relevant sexual issues many Nice Guys ponder when considering sex:

Is sex with her is the right thing to do?

Is she is attracted to me?

Is the time right for the two of us to have sex?

Are the two of us on the same page?

Will I be good enough in bed?

How many guys has she had sex with?

Is she having a sexual relationship with someone else?

These are all examples of some of the considerations Nice Guys take into account when he is interacting with someone whose feelings he cares about; who he wants to engage in sex.

To complicate matters further, the Nice Guy's consideration usually falls into two categories: sexual and nonsexual. The Nice Guy usually has to keep his eye on two balls when he is pursuing a woman sexually, one ball is how does he go about practically having sex with this woman, and the other ball is how will he manage the consequences of sex with the with the woman. Also, if or when the relationship turns sexual, he also may have concerns about how the relationship will be affected as a result of sex.

The most common concerns Nice Guys have about how the relationship or interaction will be affected because of sex include:

How will she be after sex?

Will she disrupt my life?

Will sex or pursuing sex with her be a mistake?

Will the relationship now just be sex based?

Was sex a onetime thing?

Will it adversely affect the relationship somehow?

These are just a few of the many thoughts and issues the Nice Guy considers when he is considering taking the relationship sexual.

This is another reason why the Nice Guy is vulnerable to the Jerk, and this is where he often loses the woman to the Jerk over and over again. While the Nice Guy is trying to figure out the best course of action, the Jerk only has one, and this single course of action gives him incredible efficiency. Expressing your sexual concerns when it comes to her is the best way for the Nice Guy not to dilute his sexual power. It would benefit Nice Guys greatly to understand that most women do not mind a genuine respectful expression of sexual interest, even if it is about having sex just for sake of having sex.

Let's take a spring break type event or a cruise ship as examples of what we are talking about when it comes to genuine sexual expression. Both potentially have sexually charged atmospheres filled with people from out of town who are looking for fun. Both are perfect examples of situations where both the men and women are more interested in the possibility of a one night stand, or casual sex than they probably are normally. It would be dishonest and insincere for either party to pretend otherwise. As long as both parties are honest with each other, then there should not be any problems with expressing your sexual desires.

There is nothing wrong with having sex with someone just for the sake of having sex, as long as both parties understand and agree to it. Expression of genuine sexual attraction is never wrong when done sincerely and respectfully. Women do not mind sexual expression, what they do mind is when men are not honest about their sexual intentions and are disrespectful. No one likes to be deceived. As long as your sexual desire is sincere, justified, and appropriate to your situation. then you should be fine overall.

How Nice Guy Handles the Responsibility of Initiating Sex

It would greatly benefit the Nice Guy to learn how to be more efficient in expressing his sexual desire because it is more difficult for the Nice Guy to have sex than it is for the Jerk. Part of the reason why is because of how Nice Guys go about taking on the responsibility of initiating and introducing sex into the interaction. There are many concerns and issues for the Nice Guy to consider when it comes to introducing sex into the relationship/interaction.

Some include:

Recognizing when she is ready	Bringing up sex
Touching her appropriately	Going for the first kiss
Pursuing her respectfully	Asking for sex
Planning how to have sex	Planning logistics
Expressing interest	Risking rejection
Answering her concerns/objections	Making it enjoyable

Women want their potential sexual partner to be certain in their pursuit of sex with them, and the Nice Guy, by his very nature, is rarely one hundred percent certain when it comes to the sexual pursuit of her, especially in comparison to the Jerk who is also perusing her.

Many Nice Guys have been trained to look at this particular lack of certainty as a flaw, instead of what it really is. This lack of certainty in this case is a characteristic of what happens to someone who is taking into consideration the other person with whom they want to have sex. What the Nice Guy should do is work on understanding where his lack of uncertainty comes from.

For example, many Nice Guys are afraid to initiate sex with a woman because he believes he does not know how to please her sexually. Because of this uncertainty, he will often feel bad and confuse this uncertainty with him thinking there is something wrong with him. This embarrassment will keep him from taking the necessary steps to fix that situation. If he learned to listen to his uncertainty and not fear this "negative" thought, then he would understand that his uncertainty is perfectly natural in this case. This is because if he had not had sex with her yet, then how could he know how to please her? When the Nice Guy understands why he is uncertain to initiate sex with her, then he will be in a much better position to manage his uncertainty, and express his desire.

When it comes to the responsibility of initiating sex, the Nice Guy's number one priority beyond himself, is her comfort. The most common way the Nice Guy tries to make sure she is comfortable sexually is to ask her to take up some of the pressure of the responsibility of initiating sex. This "meet me halfway approach" is how he proves to himself that she is sincerely interested in having sex with him.

Some ways Nice Guys want help women to initiate sex

Waiting for her to call

Giving him permission to kiss her

Expecting her to touch him

Waiting for her to bring up sex

Hoping she invites herself over

Waiting for her to tell him what she likes

There is nothing wrong with wanting or asking a woman to take up her share of the responsibility of sexual initiation if your reasons for doing are legit. A legitimate reason for letting her take up the responsibility includes any reason where you think her taking responsibility is best option for you two to have sex. If this is your intention, then you are OK.

Examples of legitimate reasons to let a woman initiate sex:

Because you genuinely enjoy it

It is your way of being sure she wants it

She is better at it

You want to try something different

It is how you are turned on

Nice Guys want women to take part in their own seduction, whereas the Jerk is often in complete control or more control of the seduction than the Nice Guy. This is because his main purpose is pleasing himself. This is why you have to be really effective and efficient at communicating genuine sexual desire. The most efficient way to do this is to tell her you want to please her and ask her to tell or show you how. This is not a guarantee that your will get sex from her, it is only a guarantee that you will be genuine while trying to have sex.

CONCLUSION

If I have achieved my goal, then you should be in the perfect position to start using your Nice Guy tendencies to your advantage. The reason why I say "start" is because to be a Militant Nice Guy, that is to be someone who is truly proud to be a Nice Guy, takes time. This is because understanding who you are as a Nice Guy is a process.

Often, when one comes from a motivational speech, or reads a book that inspires them to make a change, that person is often excited about how inspired they are, or how motivated they feel. They will often say things like, "I am a new man," Or, "This book changed my life," Or, "I have a new perspective on how I see things," Or, "I now have this problem in my life handled," etc. You may even feel this way after reading this book. Now what often happens is this person who was so excited at the beginning slowly starts to lose his motivation and falls back into his same old habits. This is because they have mistaken the certainty and sense of purpose that come from discovering what to do or what they want with the knowledge of how to implement it.

It is the same with understanding what it means to be a Militant Nice Guy. You now know there is a great Conspiracy working against you, and you know how and why. The issue now is that it is up to you to determine how to use this knowledge. Gaining knowledge or inspiration to act is just the beginning. It is just like your doctor telling you if you don't lose weight, then you will get diabetes. You know you need to lose weight, and a doctor telling you should be motivation enough, but inspiration or motivation is not the same as knowing what type of workout is right for you, and making a workout plan you can stick to is up to you. This is one reason why many people fail to stick to work out plans, because most people only know what they need to do, and not how they should do it in a way that is right for them. As a result their desire diminishes and they workout less and less as they become more and more overwhelmed with demands of their life.

I say this not to demoralize you, but to give you a sense of what will happen when you try to be a "new you" without knowing what to expect. Understanding who you are is a process that happens over time, rarely is there a dramatic bolt of lightning or the movie montage moment, nor is there some great ceremony announcing your great change. It involves, acquiring information, processing that information, determining what that information means for you, implementation, and repetition.

What I am trying to say is that gaining a new sense of purpose, knowledge, resolve, or insight is only the beginning of your journey. What you decide to do with that knowledge is where the real challenge begins. If you were to instantly receive fifty-thousand dollars, yes you would be happy about it, but your real challenge would be trying to determine what to do with the money. Who you are as a person, what you want to be as a person, and where you currently stand will go a long way to determining how you will use your new-found money. It is the same with being a Militant Nice Guy. It is to you to determine how to use your Nice Guy tendencies to your advantage.

Attaining new knowledge or a sense of purpose could be compared to buying a new computer. Most people are excited when they first get a computer. However, most people know that getting a new computer is only the beginning, they are excited because they can see how their lives would be better with the computer. Now when it comes to getting a new computer, most people understand that a significant part of first getting a computer is learning how to use that computer effectively. You have to go through a learning period, and a trial and error period, and only then can use the computer effectively, and even after that initial learning period, most people know they still have much to learn about their computer.

It is the same with implementing any new piece of knowledge. You now know you can use your Nice Guy tendencies to be a more effective Nice Guy, but this is only on an intellectual level. You may not yet know how to apply your new knowledge for yourself, or what it means for you practically. That is, you do not yet know exactly how to trust yourself, or how to make your Nice Guy tendencies work for your particular situations, and what role you want them to play in your life. Another reason why you will encounter some difficulty using your Nice Guy tendencies is because you do not yet know how to listen to them, this is especially true if this is your first time reading this book.

An excellent way to start to understand how to use your Nice Guy tendencies to be a better Nice Guy is to treat them just like you would treat that new computer you bought. You would examine and try out the computer to see how it worked. Then you would see how you could use the computer to enhance your life.

The first thing I would recommend, with your new understanding is to look around your world with your new perspective and examine what you see, be conscious of your feelings and thought processes. Look around your job, school, gym, bar, anywhere you spend time and see what kind of conclusions you come to on your own about what it means to be a Militant Nice Guy. After you have formed your opinions, then go out and challenge the hell out of them. Then do it again. Then do it again, and again.

Thank you,

Terrance Terry

ACKNOWLEDGMENTS

So many people have contributed to me being a better Nice Guy until it would be impossible for me to mention them all. But I would like to give a very special thanks to those special people who have contributed to *Militant Nice Guy* being a better book. Jose Brown, Norm Chong, and Jamal Rowland. Thanks this book would not be the same without you.

www.ingramcontent.com/pod-product-compliance
Lightning Source LLC
Chambersburg PA
CBHW072135020426
42334CB00018B/1807